THE FOURTH
DIMENSION
VOLUME II

Other books by **David Yonggi Cho*** available from
BRIDGE-LOGOS *Publishers*:

—Daniel
—Fourth Dimension, Volume One
—Leap of Faith
—Solving Life's Problems
—Suffering . . . Why Me?
—Successful Home Cell Groups

* DAVID YONGGI CHO
(Name changed from "Paul")

Dr. Cho's Name Change...A few days before Easter 1992,
while Dr. Cho was praying, he felt the Holy Spirit speak to him and
tell him to change his name from "Paul" Yonggi Cho to "David"
Yonggi Cho—and to spend more time at home in Korea to build
the Kingdom of God there. In obedience to the directive he received
that morning, Dr. Cho immediately obeyed and, on Easter Sunday
morning, he announced to the church family that he had changed
his name.

THE FOURTH DIMENSION

DIMENSION
VOLUME II

More Secrets for a Successful Faith Life

Dr. DAVID YONGGI CHO*
with R. Whitney Manzano, Ph.D.

Bridge-Logos *Publishers*
North Brunswick, NJ

(* Name changed from "Paul"—see opposite page)

Scripture verses marked NKJVJ are taken from the New King James Version Copyright © 1979, 1980, 1982, Thomas Nelson Publishers, Inc. Used by permission.

Scripture verses marked KJV are taken from the King James Version of the Bible.

The Fourth Dimension, Volume II
Copyright © 1983
by David Yonggi Cho
Library of Congress Catalog Card Number: 79-65588
International Standard Book Number: 088270-561X

Bridge-Logos *Publishers*
1300 Airport Road, Suite E
North Brunswick, NJ 08902

Contents

v

Introduction

In 1978 I wrote the first volume of *The Fourth Dimension*. At that time, I knew the spiritual condition of North America, but I endeavored to soften the impact of the revolutionary principles which I stated. Since then, I have gone to America often and have developed a television ministry there. I also have become much more aware of the spiritual maturity of the Christian community in America. Therefore, I have written this second volume to share in more depth and with more updated examples the principles of success that have allowed me to lead the largest single congregation in the world which now comprises over 275,000 active members.

Some might not understand what I mean when speaking of the fourth dimension. Therefore, I will try to explain briefly my use of the term.

"Dimension" is a common word used in the disciplines of physics and mathematics. In mathematics, it is a term of measurement. For example, the term "one-dimensional" would be used to indicate the extension of a line. It also indicates that whatever has only one dimension has no thickness, only length. Two dimensions would indicate the properties or extension of a plane, having length and breadth. Three dimensions would indicate not only length and breadth but also depth or thickness. In physics there is another aspect to the measurement of physical phenomena. That is time.

Sir Isaac Newton is credited with the development of many great discoveries in the field of physics. He explained the movement of planets in their orbits by the law of gravity. However, he used only three dimensions in the development of his theories.

Einstein introduced the concept of time and space as another physical dimension. Some have called this the fourth dimension. Therefore, if I use the standard three-dimensional Newtonian cosmography, I would be correct in using the fourth dimension. If I used Einstein's view of the universe, I should call it the fifth dimension.

Feeling that the importance of the truths which I am about to share overshadow scientific technicalities and knowing that I have confidence in the reader to be aware of the differences in the systems previously stated, I will retain the title I originally used, *The Fourth Dimension.*

God originally created us as physical beings. Yet, having breathed the breath of life into Adam, He gave him the capacity to understand and communicate with God in another than the physical level. He could communicate in the dimension of spirit. "God is a Spirit. They that worship God, must worship Him in spirit and truth" (John 4:24).

In Genesis 2 we see that God took the lowest and mixed it with the highest to create man. He took earth and breathed into it the breath of divine life. Everything else God created by merely commanding it to be so. Yet, when it came to man, He physically formed man after His own likeness. Since the likeness of God is Christ (John 14:9), we were created after the image of Christ.

In Genesis 2:17, God told Adam that if he disobeyed His commands he would die. He disobeyed yet continued to live and beget children with his wife, Eve. Adam did not die physically; he only died spiritually. Nonetheless, that capacity for communicating with God and understanding spiritual dimensional reality continues to exist within man till this day. After a person is regenerated by the Holy Spirit, when he accepts Christ as his Savior, he is reactivated spiritually. He is born again.

As Christians we, therefore, must become aware of spiritual reality and familiarize ourselves with the fourth dimension so that we might be as comfortable in it as we are in the three dimensional plane in which we live.

Therefore, the fourth dimension is that plane of existence where God dwells, which exists in a greater reality than the three-dimensional plane that we are all familiar with. "The lesser is always contained in the greater." We must understand that the three dimensions of physical reality are contained in the greater plane of spirit. It is possible for us to know the length, breadth, and depth of the love of God as well as all other spiritual reality. The Holy Spirit has been given to us to guide us to this new reality we experience as Christians. It is with sincere trust and confidence in Him that we endeavor to share the truths and experiences which are outlined in this book.

Preface—My Story

I was born in the southern part of Korea during the Japanese occupation. I cannot express in this chapter the untold suffering that we experienced during that time in our history.

Korea is situated between Japan and China. This unfortunate geographical position has meant that we have been the battleground of many wars between these two nations. But these circumstances have developed an independent and proud people who are proud of their heritage and language, which have been in continual existence for more than five thousand years.

My father was a hard-working man and was also very religious. In fact, he was a leading Buddhist layman in our area. Buddhism is somewhat different in Korea and Japan than in Southern Asia. We practiced a more intellectually philosophical Buddhism.

Christianity received respect from the Korean people

because of the way in which Christians suffered during World War II. Their patriotism and heroism was appreciated by all Korean people. Right after the war we began to start rebuilding our country. Many American missionaries came to help us and their assistance was never forgotten. But, not long after the war was over, the Russians encouraged the North Korean Communists to invade the South. This was called the Korean Conflict by the United Nations and was even more devastating than World War II. After the war with the North, we were totally demoralized and impoverished.

It was during this time that I had to leave school and look for work so that I might be able to help my family financially. My only hope was for survival. Some say that this instinct is man's primary motivational force. This was true of me during this time. I took any job I could get just to be able to buy food. Sometimes I held several jobs in one single day. During a normal afternoon, while I was tutoring a junior high school student, I felt very sick. My chest was heaving convulsively, and I began to vomit blood. After bleeding profusely from my mouth and nostrils, I fainted and collapsed.

After an indeterminate period of time I regained consciousness and struggled to get home. My parents had to sell their precious possessions in order to take me to the hospital so that I could be diagnosed. It did not take the doctors long to diagnose the trouble. I had advanced and terminal tuberculosis. I was now eighteen years old and dying. With no future or hope for cure, I was simply sent home to die. "You have three or four months to live," was the last thing the doctor told me as I was sent home.

"Why me?" I cried, as I lay on my straw mat in our tiny house. The calendar by my bed had only three months left on it. "Dear Buddha, won't you help me to get better and live?" I prayed daily. But nothing happened. Every day I felt weaker. I could only hope for a quick death as painless as possible. Then one day, I prayed a prayer that was to change my life. "Oh, unknown God, if you exist, please help me. If you can give me my life back, I promise you that I will spend the rest of my days serving you and helping others."

Interestingly, there is a Korean word for the One God, *Hanna-neem*. *Hanna* is our word for "one"; *neem* is a suffix used after any proper noun which means, "honorable one." The Japanese don't have a word like this in their vocabulary, so it is much more difficult for them to conceive of a single, all-powerful God.

Paul states in the first chapter of Romans that God's truth is revealed to all men. However, it is man's sinful nature that suppresses the truth of God. Therefore, there is no excusing man's ignorance of God and His laws. In preaching the gospel to those who are not aware of the God of the Bible, we simply have to state the truth in the power of the Holy Spirit. It is the Spirit's job to convince the world of God's reality. There is no question in my mind that those hours spent in silence and contemplation were not wasted. It did not take me long to lose confidence in the Buddha and begin to grope in the darkness of my knowledge for the true and living God who has been revealed in Jesus Christ.

Not long after my prayer to the One, True and Living God, a young lady came to visit me. The girl was in high school and she came after school with a large book under her arm. "I want to speak to you about Jesus Christ, Yonggi," she said. "Now you must listen to me."

"Thank you for coming, but as you know, I am a good Buddhist. Since I am about to die, I would not consider changing religions," I responded to her as kindly as I could. She did not know how upset I really was.

"That's all right," she continued. "I am going to speak to you about Jesus anyway." She then told me the life of Christ, His virgin birth, His life, His death on the cross and His resurrection. Then she told me how I could be saved by believing on Christ and accepting His forgiveness for my sins.

I listened patiently to her strange story, but when she left I was relieved. The next day, after school, there she was again. Again she told me about the love of God for sinners like me and His ability to deliver me from all my sins and torments. Well, the only torment I was concerned about was the torment of tuberculosis. But I did not say much. I just listened patiently and hoped that she would leave and leave me alone with my misery.

The rest of the week I knew that, at about three o'clock in the afternoon, I would be receiving a visit from my high school missionary telling me the same story which I did not want to hear.

Finally, after I had heard her story over and over again, I lost my patience and told her to get lost. "Please, don't tell me any more. I'm sick and tired of your persistence and foolish stories; allow me to die in peace," I screamed in desperation.

I thought that my rudeness would drive her away. But she did not leave. Instead, she simply lowered her head by my bed and began to pray for me. Then she began to cry: "Please, Jesus, forgive him. He is sick, he does not mean what he is saying," she prayed, unable to hold back the tears. The sight of her kneeling and praying before me touched me very deeply. I could not understand why she would concern herself so much for me. Why should she love me enough to cry? Who is this God that she talks about so much that would send someone to spend every afternoon talking to me and sharing the concern that she shared? Could this girl's God be the God that I prayed to when I was begging for my life?

Suddenly, I felt a strange, tingling sensation. Goose bumps were all over my body. I was scared, confused, but also challenged. "Please stop crying," I begged as I touched her head. "I'm sorry I got so angry with you. I will become a Christian for your sake." With that, she looked up at me and began to smile. Although the tears were still flowing down her cheeks, they were no longer tears of sorrow but now they were tears of joy and happiness.

"I want you to take my most prized possession," she said softly as she handed me her Bible.

I bowed politely and thanked her, the pain now rushing again through my chest. Still in pain and now coughing convulsively, I turned to Genesis 1. "Oh no, I'm afraid with the severity of your sickness, you won't be able to get past the Old Testament," she said with great concern. "You better start at Matthew."

This was the first time I had ever held a Bible in my hand. I found it rather large and cumbersome. Yet, with her assistance, I found the Gospel of Matthew, the beginning of the New Testament.

As I began to read, I became quite disappointed. " 'Abraham begat Isaac,' " I thought to myself. "What kind of religion is this?" Buddhism is quite systematic and logical. Its rituals are not hard to understand. This new religion was full of genealogy. I could not accept this kind of a boring religion. "I'm sorry, but I think this book reads too much like a telephone directory,"

I said politely as I handed her Bible back to her.

"Oh no. You can't do that," she said firmly. "Don't worry about all these Hebrew names right now. Later they will be a great blessing to you, but now read on." After she left, I began to read again through the Gospels. Although I was not challenged intellectually by the simple stories, I found myself drawn to the person of Jesus Christ.

In my terrible physical and emotional condition, I needed someone to guide me through to victory. I didn't need a new philosophy that would stimulate my mind. I needed someone who could touch my heart and my body. That someone has become the most important person in my life.

The more I read about Jesus, the more I loved Him. His compassion and love caused me to weep. How could this man suffer all of the pain of the cross for my sake?

Still struggling with pain, I knelt down as my young friend had done when she had cried over me. Then I uttered the words that would revolutionize my whole life and would affect my country: "Dear Jesus, please forgive me my sins. I am not worthy to belong to you. But if you can, accept me. I give myself to you. Please save me and heal me. Amen!" As I prayed I was unable to hold back the tears.

Suddenly, I felt clean. It was as if someone had given me a bath on the inside. I stood up and shouted, "Hallelujah! Thank you, God!"

After that experience, every morning I would pick up my Bible for breakfast and I would feast till dinner. I felt that I had to learn as much as possible, because this was God speaking directly to me. As a young man falls in love for the first time with a young lady, so I fell in love with Jesus Christ.

This love affair has intensified over the pasty twenty-nine years. Without anyone telling me, I knew I was going to live. After the pages of my calendar were gone, I was still alive. In six months, I was able to get out of my bed and I have not had trouble with tuberculosis since.

I then attended the Full Gospel Mission in Bilsan pastored by Reverend L.P. Richard and enjoyed fellowship with other Christians. My parents were understanding and soon followed their son into a relationship with Jesus Christ.

After attending Bible school, I pioneered my first church in a very poor town outside Seoul. Building a strong congregation of about six hundred people, I felt that I could settle down and enjoy my ministry. But then God told me to resign my church, go into downtown Seoul and build another church. My second church grew to a congregation of eighteen thousand and became the largest church in Korea. In 1969, God spoke to me again to resign and move to Yoido Island. Yoido was a marshy island that was being developed as the new seat of government by a young and successful vice-mayor, Il-Suk Cha. At that time he was a deacon in my church. His mother, one of my best members, had brought this man to my church. He took a real interest in my ministry. We then developed a four-acre section of land near where the new congress building was planned. Through much suffering we built a church which seats ten thousand people and is now being expanded to seat twenty-five thousand. This auditorium and numerous chapels throughout the complex allow us to seat thirty thousand per service for seven services. Soon, with the addition and closed circuit television, we will be able to seat sixty-thousand people per service for seven services. However, by next year even this will be too small. At our present growth rate, we will still need seating capacity for another eighty thousand people per Sunday by 1984.

The past twenty-five years of ministry has taught me many things. In this book I will share the key to success in building the largest single congregation in the history of Christianity.

1

The Holy Spirit and You

We are now living in the age of the Holy Spirit. We will never be able to accomplish our mission successfully in this world if we don't recognize His work.

The Old Testament described the time during which God the Father was in the foreground in the divine formative and creative work. The Father worked through the Holy Spirit, who used the prophets, priests and kings of Israel to accomplish His will. However, in the Old Testament, the prophets spoke about the coming of Jesus Christ, the Messiah, more than three hundred times. At His coming, our Lord Jesus Christ, the Son of God, became the central divine figure through which God spoke and accomplished His will. Although Jesus Christ always glorified the Father, He was still in the forefront, as was the divine plan. Yet the Holy Spirit was quietly working. For the miraculous ministry of Christ began after Christ was baptized and filled with the Holy Spirit. John the Baptist said of

Christ, "I did not know Him, but He who sent me to baptize with water said to me, 'Upon whom you see the Spirit descending and remaining on Him, this is He who baptizes with the Holy Spirit.' And I have seen and testified that this is the Son of God" (John 1:33, 34 NKJV).

After Christ's ministry was completed: By living an exemplary life, dying on the cross, and redeeming humanity from sin; He was resurrected and He ascended to the Father. Christ then gave the Holy Spirit His mission which is to both the world and the church.

Since the day of Pentecost, the Holy Spirit has been with us for nearly two thousand years. His presence is in the world, the church and inside every Christian. In this age of the Church, God the Father and God the Son has chosen to work through the Holy Spirit. This does not mean that I am trying to define the Trinity in too sharp a fashion—the Father, Son and the Holy Spirit are One God. Yet God is manifested in three Persons. The point that I am making is that this age is the age in which the Holy Spirit is in the forefront in His work in the earth.

If we as Christians desire to do the work of God, then this desire has been placed within us by the Holy Spirit. Yet, as a divine person, we must learn to come into a personal relationship with Him. We just cannot depend upon our theological knowledge of God. We must learn to know Him. As we grow in our consciousness of the Holy Spirit, we develop a fellowship (koinonia) with Him.

In order to better understand the person with whom we desire to have a relationship, we must know something about Him. Without learning about the Holy Spirit, we shall never be able to learn about the fourth dimension. For it is the Holy Spirit that brings us into fourth-dimensional living.

What is the Holy Spirit like?

Since we have a clear record of God the Father sharing His thoughts with the prophets, priests and kings in the Old Testament, and because we can relate to what a father is, we can have a general idea of what the Father is like. Jesus also revealed the Father in His life and teaching. The Holy Spirit has come to reveal Christ: "He will glorify Me, for He will take of what is Mine and declare it to you" (John 16:14). Therefore, the Holy Spirit takes the record in the Scriptures concerning Christ and enlightens not only His teaching but also the Son's personality. Yet the Holy Spirit's personality is not clearly and consistently referred to in the Old and New Testaments. We mainly see His work, but because of His function as a glorifier of the Son, He does not point to himself.

Since the Holy Spirit never takes physical form in the scriptural record, we cannot describe His appearance.

We can only know Him in terms of His characteristics in our souls and spirits. The only clue to a physical characteristic is found in Scripture when the Holy Spirit descended upon Jesus like a dove. The reason He chose the dove as a symbol of His presence is due to the dove's gentle nature. The Holy Spirit's gentleness is also understood when we realize that the only un- pardonable sin is that of sinning against the Holy Spirit.

Paul alludes to the Holy Spirit's nature when he tells the Ephesians, "And do not grieve the Holy Spirit of God, by whom you were sealed for the day of redemption"(Eph. 4:30, NKJV). Since the Spirit is living the life of Christ within the Christian, He has been associated not only with our faith but also with our actions. Then Paul goes on to describe the actions that will grieve the Holy Spirit: "Let all bitterness, wrath, anger, clamor, and evil speaking be put away from you, with all malice" (Eph. 4:31, NKJV). In verse 32, Paul then describes the actions which are characteristic of the Holy Spirit's nature and which thus please Him: "And be kind to one another, tenderhearted, forgiving one another, just as God in Christ also forgave you." Paul also reveals how we are to live in such obedience that we do not quench the Holy Spirit. Interestingly, the source of God's dynamic power, who has the ability to form the earth and move mountains, can be limited by the Christian's disobedience.

The Lord Jesus calls the Holy Spirit the Spirit of Truth. We know, therefore, that the Holy Spirit is full of truth and that His function within us includes to lead and guide us into all truth. This is a part of His nature. He is also called the Spirit of Wisdom, the Spirit of Understanding, the Spirit of Knowledge, and the Spirit of Judgment. Therefore, the way we are enlightened is to have a relationship with the Holy Spirit, who will impart His nature to us. For it is true that we will become like the one we fellowship with.

Three Levels of Relationship

Jesus told us that He would be with us, in us and upon us. Therefore there are three distinctive levels of relationship with the Holy Spirit.

1. *The Holy Spirit is with us.*

Since the Holy Spirit is the wind of God, we must understand how the Holy Spirit functions as God's wind (*pneuma*).

The metaphor of wind is used to describe the Holy Spirit because wind is felt and not seen. Wind can also be either powerful or gentle. The wind is also experienced everywhere in the world at the same time. Therefore the Holy Spirit is at work in accord with God's desires everywhere in the world. By sending the Holy Spirit, Jesus could break the limitations of having to be in one place at one time. Now, through the work of the Holy Spirit, He is able to effect His will and presence everywhere. We never need to look for the Holy Spirit; in fact, the Holy Spirit seeks us everywhere.

Since the Holy Spirit was sent to the world and not only to the Christian, we must understand the Holy Spirit's role in dealing with the world. Jesus said, "And when He has come, He will convict the world of sin, and of righteousness and of judgment; of sin, because they do not believe in Me; of righteousness, because I go to My Father and you see Me no more; of judgment, because the ruler of this world is judged" (John 16:8-11, NKJV). Therefore, the reason why we were convicted of our sins and desired to have Jesus Christ come into our lives as our personal savior is because the Holy Spirit was working with us. Jesus told His disciples that the Holy Spirit was with them, but in the new birth, He would be in them (John 14:17). Yet once we receive Jesus Christ as our personal Savior, we are washed by His blood and then we become ready for the Holy Spirit to move inside us.

2. *The Holy Spirit is inside us.*

The way we can accomplish the will of God is because the power to perform His will is within us, the Holy Spirit. "Then I will sprinkle clean water on you, and you shall be clean; I will cleanse you from all your filthiness and from all your idols. I will give you a new heart and put a new spirit within you; I will take the heart of stone out of your flesh and give you a heart of flesh. I will put My Spirit within you and cause you to walk in My statutes, and you will keep My judgments and do them. Then you shall dwell in the land that I gave to your fathers; you shall be My people, and I will be your God"(Ezek. 36:25-28, NKJV). In this passage of Scripture, the prophet reveals the new covenant to His people. In the past, Israel had been given commandments and had been told to live according to them. But now the Lord would do a new thing. He would wash them clean and then place within His people a new heart, one that would desire to do His will. This would be accomplished by placing His Holy Spirit within them so that He would live out His life through them. Of course, we realize that this was accomplished when Christ sent the Holy Spirit to His disciples and they experienced the new birth.

3. *The Holy Spirit is upon us.*

"But you shall receive power when the Holy Spirit is come upon you; and you shall be witnesses to Me in Jerusalem, and in all Judea and Samaria, and to the end of the earth" (Acts 1:8).

Luke tells us that Christ responded to the disciples' desire to have political power by telling them of a more important power they would receive after Pentecost. They would have the power to be witnesses. Their witness would not be limited to just the area they had grown familiar with, but would be unto the ends of the earth. This new power would be known after they had experienced the Holy Spirit coming upon them. This promise of divine power (*dunamos*) is also called experiencing the fullness of the Holy Spirit.

We therefore understand that the Holy Spirit comes to us on three different levels. He is with us (conviction of sin); He is in us (new birth) and He is upon us (in fullness).

By experiencing the Holy Spirit on these three levels, we can have not only a personal friendship with the Holy Spirit, but we can also learn to work together with Him. Can we be satisfied with just a judicial experience? No! Since the Holy Spirit is a person, He must be experienced in a personal way.

Jesus said that the Holy Spirit would not be a temporary comforter, but He would be with us forever; we can therefore spend the rest of our Christian lives with the third member of the Trinity, being changed into the image of Christ. *The Living Bible* states: "But we Christians have no veil over our faces; we can be mirrors that brightly reflect the glory of the Lord. As the Spirit of the Lord works within us, we become more and more like Him" (2 Cor. 3:18).

In a day full of theory and theology concerning God and His love, people are left cold in the pew because what they are taught has no experiential element. This experiential level only comes through fellowshiping with the Holy Spirit. How do we learn to fellowship and have intimate communion with the Holy Spirit? There are four steps I have followed in developing this relationship which has revolutionized my life and ministry:

1. *The Development of* Koinonia *(Fellowship) with the Holy Spirit.*

To have communion with a person we must have fellowship. To have fellowship we must share our feelings, knowledge or will together through expression in words. We cannot just keep our feelings of love in our minds, they must be shared. When we want to have a relationship with the Holy Spirit, we must learn how to adore Him and thank Him! We should learn how to pray in the Holy Spirit; we should welcome His presence and show our appreciation for Him. Without doing this we can never develop fellowship. As long as He is not recognized, He will not push himself on us because of His gentle nature. Yes, the Holy Spirit is a gentleman.

The New Testament church experienced the Holy Spirit in a dynamic way. "As they ministered to the Lord, and fasted, the Holy Ghost said, 'Separate me Barnabas and Saul for the work whereunto I have called them' " (Acts 13:2, KJV). It is obvious that the Holy Spirit was given the credit for speaking and calling men to labor in the new harvest fields.

Yes, the Holy Spirit, who is the Lord of the Harvest, chooses His laborers. That is the reason we should take the Holy Spirit as our supreme Lord of the Harvest in our churches and give Him the recognition He rightly deserves. He is the administrator of the love of God and the grace of the Lord Jesus Christ.

I have learned how to develop this fellowship in my life. In 1964, by God's direct intervention, I found out that I should develop a deep fellowship with the Holy Spirit. Up until that time I recognized the Holy Spirit only as an experience, but God sharply rebuked me because I had neglected fellowship with the Holy Spirit. Since then, I determined to have intimate fellowship with the Holy Spirit. Before going into a service, I began to say, "Dear Holy Spirit, let's go and preach." After getting to the meeting, I would dwell in His presence and, having been announced, I would say, "Now, Holy Spirit, this is the time to preach, so let us give forth the Word of God together." After my message, I would say, "Holy Spirit, you did a great job today. I was blessed by your word."

In my office, as I prepared my messages, I would say quietly, "Dear Holy Spirit, let's read this word you wrote together. Now please, open my eyes to see Thy truth so I may teach your people how to live." Before retiring, I would say, "Good night, Holy Spirit, we have had a great day together." The first thing that I would do when I woke up the next morning was to say, "Good morning, Holy Spirit, together we are going to bring the message of Jesus Christ to this lost and dying world. You cannot fail. Therefore, I cannot fail."

I did not just turn to the Holy Spirit in time of trouble, I learned how to walk in the Holy Spirit as a natural way of life.

2. *The Development of Partnership with the Holy Spirit.*

We must realize that we are to be in partnership with the Holy Spirit. We understand the concept of partnership in a business. When two or more people get together to form a business, they must have very close contact with each other. Not only must they have communion, but they must also be in business to make a profit. No one goes into business to lose money. If a business does not show a profit after a reasonable period of time, then it will go bankrupt.

We are in God's business. We are in business to make a profit, not in money, but in souls. There are many churches throughout the world that are not making a profit in God's business. Many churches are sitting nearly vacant, year after year.

On a recent trip through Europe I was amazed at some beautiful cathedrals that were sitting absolutely vacant. Some were being used as factories and warehouses. My heart was broken when I saw all these unused buildings that were once dedicated to God. I only wished I had some of those buildings in Korea. We would have them full of Christians.

The reason so much of God's work shows little or no profit is because of the partnership arrangement. I am convinced that there is no vineyard too hard, no field too barren, no area too difficult for the Holy Spirit to be successful.

When you are in partnership with the Holy Spirit, He brings all of the finances, all of the grace and all of the love into the partnership. After all, the Holy Spirit is the senior partner; we are only junior partners. The junior partner's responsibility is to listen to the senior partner. The senior partner makes the strategy and the junior partner carries it out.

The Apostle Paul is a prime example. Paul had been fervent in his desire to persecute the Christians, believing that they were a false sect of the Jewish faith. While on his way to imprison followers of Jesus Christ, he was arrested by the Lord. He then wanted to work for God. Luke reports: "And straightway he preached Christ in the synagogues, that he is the Son of God" (Acts 9:20, KJV).

The Jews, however, tried to kill him. So Paul disputed with the Gentiles, but they also tried to destroy him. So the church decided to send him back to Tarsus, his hometown.

After Paul had left the area, Luke says, "Then had

the churches rest throughout all Judaea and Galilee and Samaria . . ."(Acts 9:31, KJV). Paul had desire and ability. He was also trained in religion and logic, yet more was needed for success than just ability and training. Paul had to learn to go into partnership with the Holy Spirit.

In Acts 16, we read of an experience Paul had which would completely revolutionize his life and ministry. After having a successful ministry throughout Asia Minor there arose a series of problems that could have caused Paul to give up. Yet out of the trial of his faith, God developed a new strategy for His ministry that has literally changed history.

Barnabas was not only his close friend and partner in the ministry, but he was also the man that caused Paul to be accepted by the other apostles in Jerusalem. He was a formerly wealthy man that had given all to the church and was willing to sacrifice everything for the work of God. Barnabas' nephew, John Mark, who would later write one of the four Gospels, was repentant regarding his past failure, when he had given up the ministry and left the apostolic team. Paul did not want to take John Mark on the new journey which would cover the same ground as before, but Barnabas was more forgiving. He wanted to give the young man another chance. The argument between Barnabas and Paul was so strong that they decided to part company and go their separate ways.

Paul then chose Timothy, who was half Greek, and went on what he thought was a regular trip to re-establish the same churches that had already been built. Paul had used prayer and logic in planning his itinerary, but the Holy Spirit had something much larger for Paul than he could ever imagine. Without Paul realizing it, Timothy was the perfect man for his future ministry to the Gentiles. Paul tried to return home by going the route through Asia, but the Holy Spirit forbade him. Then he decided that he should go to Bithynia, but the Holy Spirit said, "No!" So Paul went down to the coastal town of Troas, not knowing what to do next. Then the Holy Spirit showed Paul a vision of a European calling to him for help. Did the Holy Spirit want them to preach the gospel to heathen Europe? If the answer was yes, then it would be a great change in the apostolic strategy, yet part of the plan of God.

Through Europe, the gospel has come to America and the rest of the world.

Paul learned that he had to surrender his strategy to the Holy Spirit in a partnership arrangement in order for him to be successful in the King's business. We also must be trained to wait on the Holy Spirit and hear His voice. As the early apostles learned the secret of partnership with the Holy Spirit, they built the church successfully in the first two centuries. How can you see your life flourish successfully? By taking the Holy Spirit as your senior partner.

3. *Transportation in the Holy Spirit.*

It has been said that the progress of a civilization can be measured by the volume of its transportation system. This is the age of quick and massive transportation. Seemingly, the world has become smaller because we are now able to travel completely around the world at phenomenal speeds using the latest means of transportation.

I have discovered that in order for us to have a successful Christian life, we must learn how to have a transportation or "moving together" with the Holy Spirit. What is the Holy Spirit's transportation system? The Holy Spirit transports the love and grace of God to us and then takes our prayers and supplications and transports them back to God.

"Then another angel, having a golden censer, came and stood at the altar. And he was given much incense that he should offer it with the prayers of all the saints, and upon the golden altar which was before the throne. And the smoke of the incense, with the prayers of the saints, ascended before God from the angel's hand" (Rev. 8:3, 4, NKJV).

There are great obstacles to having prayers answered. Daniel discovered that prayers can be hindered by spiritual forces opposed to God. Yet the way to have prayers rise to God quickly without any hindrance is to have them anointed by the Holy Spirit. Without this anointing, prayers can be hindered, but nothing can stop the transportational system of the Holy Spirit.

"And hope maketh not ashamed; because the love of God is shed abroad in our hearts by the Holy Ghost which is given unto us" (Rom. 5:5, KJV). Why are we not disappointed when our hope is in God? Because of the transportational system of the Holy Spirit which takes the love of God and fills our heart with it.

4. *The Unity of the Holy Spirit.*

We are joined with the Holy Spirit when we receive Jesus Christ as our personal Savior; therefore, we can no longer consider ourselves as individuals apart from the Holy Spirit. We should be aware of the Holy Spirit being an intimate part of us, and that we are one with Him. I like to think of our relationship with the Holy Spirit in very practical human terms: we are actually living with the Holy Spirit, sleeping together, awakening together, eating together, doing our work together, and praying together.

If we don't maintain this consciousness of being together with the Holy Spirit, then our work is empty and unfulfilled. We must remember that whatever we do, God is measuring the work we do for Him in a qualitative, not quantitative way. The fruit of our human flesh cannot be accepted in heavenly places. Only the work which is done by the power of the Holy Spirit can be acceptable in the Kingdom of God. Therefore, we must have a divine union with the Holy

Spirit. If we desire that our fruit remain, or be lasting, we cannot forget that that fruit is the fruit of the Holy Spirit.

Now that we have studied the essential fact of learning how to live with the Holy Spirit, we can learn to use the principle of incubation.

Incubation

When we read Genesis, we find out a very interesting Scripture. Genesis 1:2 says, "And the earth was without form, and void; and darkness was upon the face of the deep. And the Spirit of God moved upon the face of the waters."

When the whole earth was in a state of chaos, the Spirit of the Lord was upon the water. The words "upon the waters" literally mean the Holy Spirit was "fluttering" over the water, or the Holy Spirit was "incubating" over the water. Another word with the same thought is the word "brooding." The whole world, previously in a state of chaos, was incubated by the Holy Spirit. Then the word of creation was given and a new world came into being.

To have a creatively victorious life, we must learn the principle of incubation. In order to understand this principle, we can look at a very simple example of the chicken and the egg. I am not interested in the proverbial question of which came first. No. I just want to point out the obvious fact that in order to have more chickens, one must have eggs. When a mother hen lays her eggs, she has to sit on them, or incubate them, so that the eggs will hatch and become baby chicks.

In Hebrews 11:1, we see how the Holy Spirit uses our cooperation for faith to be produced. "Faith is the substance of things hoped for, the evidence of things not seen."

There are four major points that we can learn that will help us in following the Holy Spirit's example in incubation. As we learn these points, our lives will be revolutionized. We will become more creative and imaginative.

1. In order for us to incubate, we must have a clear goal. "Faith is the substance of *things* . . . ." In this verse, "things" is comparable to the egg which we previously mentioned. You cannot begin to incubate without having something you desire to see come to pass. You must have a clear-cut idea in your mind as your goal is before you. This idea must be one which the Holy Spirit has placed in your mind. This "egg" (thing) must fill your heart and imagination. Your heart has to be filled with the desire; the Holy Spirit will answer us based upon the desires of our hearts.

Just as we were in Christ, before the worlds were founded, God had a clear goal of why He wanted the Holy Spirit to incubate this world. He wanted us to inhabit this planet and fill it. He wanted the human race to glorify Him. He wanted this earth as a place where

He could send His Son to redeem not only humanity, but all creation. This earth then becomes the central stage upon which the mighty power of God will work and will bring forth His glory to all creation.

May I ask you, the reader, a personal question at this time? What is the desire of your heart right now? Is your desire for someone in your family to come to Christ?

Then I need to ask you further how great that desire is. Are you moved to tears thinking about your son or daughter accepting Christ as Savior? Have you ever dreamed about your son having such fervency in God's love that he is actually winning others to Christ?

If your answer to this question is yes, then that desire has been placed there by the Holy Spirit. That desire is like an egg, ready to be incubated. Of course the example can work for any other desire placed within us by the Holy Spirit.

Jesus said, "Verily I say unto you, whosoever shall say to *this mountain* [a clearly defined objective—not any mountain, but *this* mountain] be thou removed and be thou cast into the sea, and shall not doubt in his heart but shall believe that those things which he says shall come to pass, he shall have *whatsoever* he *says*."

Therefore, we should have a clear-cut goal when we pray, or when we incubate. Without this goal our prayers are aimless and the meditation in our heart will go nowhere.

The Fourth Dimension

I have learned this principle since the beginning of my life and ministry. I was in one of the poorest areas of Korea. I fasted and prayed, not because of my great spirituality but because I had nothing to eat. Being single at that time, I was living in a small room. The room was so cold during the winter that I had to wrap myself with blankets in order to stay alive. Yet people were getting saved in our little tent church.

In my small room, all I had was a bare floor. I had no desk, nor did I have a chair or means of transportation. So I began to pray for a desk and a chair and a bicycle. When I first started asking God for these items, I thought that immediately someone would open my door and give me the three items which I had ordered. Months went by and still nothing happened. During that time, I got very discouraged and told the Lord, "Dear Lord, you know how poor we are here. Yet I have told these people that they can have confidence in you to provide for their needs. Now, all I have been asking for is for you to give me three things that I really need. I have been asking and asking, but you have not given me anything. Perhaps you are going to take a long time to answer me; after all, time means nothing to you. But if you wait until I die, then I won't need a chair, desk and bicycle."

In my discouragement, I began to cry. Then the peace of God settled on me. (Whenever I sense His divine presence I know God is trying to speak to my heart.) I got very quiet and began to listen. As I settled my emotions and opened my spiritual ears, I heard the still, small voice of God: "My son, I heard your prayer when you first prayed four months ago."

"So where," I yelled out, "is my answer?"

"Your trouble, my son, is that you do what so many of my children do. When you give me your requests, they are so vague that I cannot answer them. Don't you realize that there are dozens of chairs, many kinds of desks with differing woods, and many makes of bicycles? Why aren't you more specific?"

This was the turning point of my life. Now I had the key to getting my prayers answered. I then started asking myself, "Why didn't the professors in Bible College teach me how to pray effectively?" Then I thought, "Perhaps they did not realize this principle themselves."

"Now, what should I ask for specifically?" I asked myself. I then prayed, "Heavenly Father, I would like to have a desk made out of Philippine mahogany. My desk is going to be large enough for me to be able to lay out all of my study books along with my Bible. As far as my chair is concerned, I would like to have one with a steel frame so that it is sturdy and one with the little wheels on the bottom so I can roll around like a big shot executive." I smiled as I thought of myself rolling around on a chair in a room like the one I was living in.

When it came time to ask about my bicycle, I gave it some more thought then asked, "Father, the bicycle is to be one made in the U.S.A." At that time there were German bicycles, Japanese bicycles and Korean ones. However, I knew that the United States made the strongest ones. Yet this would take extra faith, because American products were very expensive and rare in Korea at that time.

When I woke up the next morning, I did not feel any great anointing in my heart. It wasn't the same as the night before when God had spoken to me. In fact, I was still struggling with discouragement. How easy it is to believe God when His presence is so obvious. But, when we return to normal, our faith level goes down and it is hard to stand upon the promise we received when our faith level was very high. This is the time to know that we do not stand on promises made to us in prayer, but we must stand on the Word of God in the Scriptures. I then opened my Bible and my eyes fell on Romans 4:17: "God raises the dead and calls those things which be not as if they were."

My confession was very important. If God calls those things which are not as if they were, why couldn't I do the same thing? God calls us complete in Christ, yet as we look at ourselves and one another, we appear anything but complete. Why can God call me complete if I don't feel complete, look complete or act in a complete way? Because God sees us in Christ. He does not look at us as we are, but He judges us as we shall be. God practices a principle which we must learn to follow. He does not look at the present circumstances, but He sees the end from the beginning and speaks as if all He is working on is already finished.

I learned that once I had prayed specifically and had received the assurance that my prayers had been heard, I had to then visualize the answer and begin to speak as if it had already taken place.

During the meeting, I shared my experience and began to tell the people about my new chair, desk and bicycle. Knowing how poor we were, many people in the congregation were amazed that I had come into such great possessions. Three of the young men asked if they could come to my room and see the three things that God had given me. Then my heart stopped.

"What am I going to do, Lord?" I thought. "When they come to my room and see it is vacant as it was yesterday they are going to lose faith in my word and I might as well pack up and leave town. Nobody will ever trust me again."

When the young men came, they noticed that all I had in the room was the small mattress on the floor where I slept. So they asked me, "Pastor, where is the desk, chair and especially the American bicycle?" However, I found myself speaking prophetically to them:

"When you were in the womb, did you exist?" I asked them now with complete confidence.

"Yes," they answered.

"Could anyone see you?" I continued.

"Obviously not," they retorted.

"Then you were not visible," I stated confidently, knowing that they were finally getting my point. "Last night while I was in communion with the Holy Spirit, I conceived the chair, desk and bicycle. They are not visible yet, but they do exist. Just like you were not obvious until you were born. You see, I am now pregnant with these three items. I am calling those things which God has revealed to me that I have received (although they are not obvious) as if they were obvious," I stated, not expecting their response.

With that, they began to laugh and said, "Pastor, you are the first man in history who ever became pregnant." Even worse, the news spread around town. People would come to my church just to see the first pregnant man in history. They would come and just stare at my stomach. I was tall and very skinny, so that made me even more the object of ridicule.

"Pastor, look how big you are getting. When do you think you will be giving birth?" teased a group of youngsters outside the church one Sunday afternoon. I did not like teasing, but I knew in my heart that I had discovered an important spiritual principle that was destined to be a great blessing in my ministry in months to come.

After several months had passed I received all three of those items, exactly as I had requested them. I was given a Philippine mahogany desk, and a Mitsubishi chair with the little wheels on the bottom. And an American missionary gave me his son's slightly used American bicycle. From that time until this, I have never again prayed in vague terms. I have prayed specifically and expected God to answer me in the same way. And He has!

2. We should know how to visualize the end result of our goal. Just as a hen dreams the chick out of the egg, so we should clearly see the end result of our goal, in our vision and dream.

"Faith is the substance of things *hoped* for." When you hope for certain things then you can only have a strong vision or dream for that which you have hoped for. If you have not visualized clearly in your heart exactly what you hope for, it cannot become a reality to you. This is because you don't know yourself what you really desire the Lord to do for you. The things you really hope for can only be possessed as you visualize them clearly in your heart and mind. When they are clear in your mind the deep desire for God to grant that request now becomes a vision in your heart as well as a prayer. You will dream about it day in and day out as you are in prayer and as you go about your daily work. Without visualizing them you cannot have those things in the realm of the "hoped for."

Romans 1:17 says, "God raised the dead and called those things which be not as if they were." Because God's promises are true, all of the "hoped for" things are a reality in His plan for His children. The next step is for His children to incubate those "hoped for" things in visions and dreams. How? Dare to place that "hoped for" desire in your heart, which the Holy Spirit placed there, in a completed stage as if it has already taken place and the answer were finished. Dream it as "completed." Thank God for the total victory as "completed." As you visualize this in prayer and apply Romans 1:17, your faith will grow to believe God all the way to the final reality of that dream or vision! God is a good God! Hath He not promised and shall He not make it good? Have faith in God. Dare to believe!

What if we don't visualize the answer to our prayer? If we do not, we may not know the fullness of joy when God does answer, because we may not know if it was a direct answer to our prayer or not. We've got to learn how to use our visions and dreams. We can begin to learn by using our faith to visualize and dream the answer as being completed, as we go to the Lord in prayer. We should always try to visualize the end result as we pray. In that way, with the power of the Holy Spirit, we can incubate that which we want God to do for us.

We see a lot of these experiences in the Old Testament. God used this process of visualizing the situation to help Abraham. Abraham was ninety-nine, and Sarah his wife was ninety, years old. God wanted to give them a son but they, because of their great age, greatly doubted that it could happen. In the middle of the night, God called Abraham out from his tent and asked him to count the stars. While he was counting the stars they became innumerable to him. Then God said, "Your children shall be as innumerable as those stars." By that associated thought (seeing the stars as faces), Abraham could see the faces of his children in that night sky! By that visualization through the associated thought Abraham could see his children in visions and dreams and possess those children as a present happening in his own heart. And through that visualization he could incubate his children and dispel the doubts from his heart.

We can see that same thing happening in many places in the Old Testament and also in the New Testament, but the main thing is that we should know the importance of visualization.

In my own personal ministry in 1958, when I came out to the slum area in Seoul to start a church it was not easy. I put up an old American marine tent with a few rice mats strewn around on the floor as our sitting area for the congregation, I began to preach the gospel. Very, very few people came to hear my preaching and I was very discouraged. But when I prayed at that time suddenly my spirit would be lifted up and I could see in visions and dreams what God would do for our small church. I could see three thousand people. I could see those faces clearly in my heart. I could see the goal of three thousand in my spiritual vision and dream. I could clearly visualize them. I was finally completely possessed with that vision and dream and I was living and acting as if I had already received that many converts to minister to. Every week I was preaching like that and acting like that! By 1964 my church had three thousand members!

When you have visions and dreams like that they will bring a tremendously strong desire to see those visions and dreams all the way into reality! You know, to have a successful ministry you need this kind of powerful desire. You can only have this kind of desire aroused in you through your clear-cut vision and dream. God responds to those dreams too. Psalms 37:4 says, "Delight yourself also in the Lord and He shall give you the desires of your heart!"

3. After having a vision you must pray fervently to have the substance. Faith is the "substance." To make faith substantial you must have the assurance in your heart. "Substance" in the Greek is *nupostasis* or "the title deed." Just as if you own a piece of property you have its title deed, you should have such an assurance in your heart that excludes all doubts about the fulfillment of that goal and vision which you have already incubated. So, when you have a clear-cut goal and have

those things in the visions and dreams, then you have to pray until your faith rises up to become the "substance." Sometimes it will take a short time for the assurance to come; sometimes it will take a long time to pray through. When God gives you the assurance suddenly in your spirit you will know that you know that you have your desire, and that it is only a matter of time until you see it in reality! That is a tremendous thing!

God wants us to be specific in our prayers. Jesus passed by Jericho on His way to Jerusalem, we are told in the Gospel according to Mark. On the side of the road was a beggar, Bartimaeus, who was totally blind. He cried out to Jesus, "Jesus, son of David, have mercy on me." Others told him to be quiet, but he cried out the louder. Jesus called him out of the crowd and asked, "What do you want me to do for you?" Jesus saw that he was blind, but He wanted him to make a specific request. When Bartimaeus asked specifically for his sight, the Lord healed him.

I was preaching in a foreign country. The pastor of the church asked me if I would agree to pray for a woman in his church. She was a lovely lady, over thirty and had never been married.

"What do you want me to pray for?" I asked.

"I want to have a husband," she responded very shyly.

"What kind of a husband do you want? There are many kinds of men," I said to her.

"Well, I'll take any man that the Lord wants to give me," she answered. I told her that God does not answer vague prayers. She had prayed for many years for a husband and her prayers had not been answered because God wanted to give her a husband that would be according to her desire, not just any man.

I asked her to sit down. Giving her a piece of paper and a pen, I asked her to write down the numbers one through ten. She did.

"I'm going to ask you ten questions about the man you want and I want you to write each answer down by each number," I continued. "Number one: Is he European, Asian or African?" I asked.

"European," she said.

"Number two: How tall should he be?"

"Six feet."

"Number three: What is his profession?"

"School teacher."

"Number four: What is his main hobby?"

"Music," she continued.

On we went until she had written down ten traits describing this man that God was going to give her to marry. I then told her to take the paper home, hang it up by her mirror and look at it every day. She did.

Every day, as she prayed, she prayed specifically for this one man. She visualized him and became strong in her faith. She knew that God would provide him for her. One year later as I passed by the town I called the same pastor.

"Dr. Cho, you must come to my house for lunch today," the pastor said. When I arrived the first thing he said to me was, "She is married! She is married!"

"Who is married?" I asked.

"The old maid you prayed for," he continued. He then went on to tell me the story.

An American high school teacher had come by the church and had sung in the services during a special series of meetings. He was tall, slender and very handsome. All the young girls were interested in him, but he did not seem to pay them much attention. However, when the single lady came that I had prayed for, he immediately took an interest. They went out to dinner and by the end of that week he had proposed. No one had said anything about the ten-point list on her wall by the mirror. But, when she saw him and learned more about him she knew that this was God's answer to her prayers.

Interestingly, I received word from an unmarried Japanese girl who had read this story and began to practice praying specifically for her husband. She put up her ten-point list by her wall and within a few months she was married, too. She wrote me and told me that God had answered her prayer when she prayed specifically, having visualized her answer.

This is not a guarantee to all single ladies in the

world. However, these stories of people that I have mentioned signify the results of praying to God with a clear goal and then visualizing the answer from God, even before it comes.

4. To have a successful incubation you must release your faith power through your mouth confession. In Genesis, when the Holy Spirit had been incubating on the chaotic world, then the Word of God was released. It was exactly like that. When you have the substance, when your faith becomes substantial, you've got to release that substance through your mouth. You've got to confess that it is going to be just as your faith reassured you! By confessing you can have a tremendous thing happen. Concerning salvation the Bible clearly says, in Romans 10:9-10, *"That if thou shalt confess with thy mouth the Lord Jesus, and shalt believe in thine heart that God hath raised him from the dead, thou shalt be saved. For with the heart man believeth unto righteousness; and with the mouth confession is made unto salvation."*

Also in Mark 11:23-24, "For verily I say unto you, That whosoever shall *say* to this mountain, Be thou removed, and be thou cast into the sea; and shall not doubt in his heart, but shall believe that those things which he *saith* shall come to pass; *he shall have whatsoever he saith."*

Only by mouth confession can faith power be released allowing tremendous things to happen. As you see, you have to have a definite incubation period with the Holy Spirit. Without having this incubation it is impossible to have great things happen in our life. Many people are neglecting this part of the technique of their prayer life, and many others do not know ". . . those things which he saith shall come to pass; he shall have whatsoever he saith" (Mark 11:24, KJV).

God has taught me this valuable truth in my own experience. Nowadays, without having this period of incubation I do not dare to *speak* or to *say* what I would like to have created in my life because now I know that greater things cannot be created in my life unless I have that period of incubation.

Since 1980, I've been incubating for half a million members in our church. By the help of the Holy Spirit and prayer I've set a goal of arriving at half a million membership by 1984. That goal became my "egg," but in my vision and dreams I began to incubate that goal. I placed that goal in my vision and I began to dream and visualize that many members as if I already had them in our church. I have been incubating those goals day in and day out. I've been incubating those numbers for the glory of God twenty-four hours a day! Of course I have been praying fervently, and now I have this assurance. My faith has become substantial, and that is the reason why I am boldly declaring that we already have half a million members, and we will "see" them by 1984. In my heart, in the realm of visions and dreams I already have half a million members. Just as the time flows, the incubated goal is going to be hatched successfully.

2
The Fourth Dimension

My present understanding of the fourth dimension came through an experience I had in Korea. An old woman moved into downtown Seoul and claimed that she had been given the power to heal the sick. Many people went to her for prayer with some successful results. Even some genuine Christians were fooled by her and allowed themselves to be prayed for.

Realizing that she did not give credit to God for her power, discerning that her spirit did not confess Jesus Christ as Lord, I knew that the woman was not from God. Therefore, I told my church members to stay away from her. The Bible teaches us to test the spirits: "Beloved, do not believe every spirit, but test the spirits, whether they are of God; because many false prophets have gone out into the world. By this you know the Spirit of God: Every Spirit that confesses that Jesus Christ has come in the flesh is of God, and every spirit that does not confess that Jesus Christ has come in the flesh is not of God. And this is the spirit of the Antichrist, which you have heard was coming, and is now already in the world" (1 John 4:1-3, NKJV).

Although John was specifically referring to the heretical Docetic and Corinthian Gnostics, this Scripture is applicable today. Many false prophets are rampant throughout the whole world in increasing numbers. Christians are admonished in the first verse to test the spirits and not believe someone is from God by merely accepting their claim to divine inspiration.

"But pastor, why is this woman able to heal people?" asked a bewildered man in our church. This question caused me to go to prayer. I began to pray with my Bible by my side and began to ask God to give me the correct answer.

The question of miracles performed by people who do not represent Jesus Christ may not be as relevant to the West as it is here in Korea, but I have been faced with this same dilemma for many years. We have seen Buddhist monks performing miracles. Practitioners of Yoga have been healed of several diseases through the practice of meditation. Japanese Sokagakkai are reputed to heal the sick in their meetings. I was confused, but I approached God with the question in full confidence that He would give me the understanding.

I have discovered that prayer is the answer to dilemmas that Christians face. It takes several hours to clear your mind from all the hindrances of the world around you. However, once your mind has been cleared, you will then be able to hear the "still, small voice" of God speaking.

After several days, the answer came. The Holy Spirit revealed to me the nature of the new dimension of reality I had been born into when I became a Christian. The first three dimensions are the boundaries which govern the material world. However, there is a greater dimension which governs and includes the lesser. That dimension is the realm of spirit, the fourth dimension. The superior nature of the fourth dimension was made clear to me when I read Genesis 1:2.

Genesis is not a history book, but its history or recorded events are accurate. It is not a science book; however, its science is perfect. Genesis shows God revealing to Moses, and through Moses to us, the beginnings of this earth, its living creatures and, most importantly, man, with whom He will be forever linked in Christ.

Concerning the universe, He simply states that He created it. That's all. No detailed explanations are necessary because God is interested in developing the main theme of the book. He begins in verse 2 with a chaotic, uninhabitable world. Yet, as stated in the first chapter, the Holy Spirit brings order out of chaos. The three-dimensional plane of present existence was brought into order by a divine act moving in a greater dimension. The Holy Spirit was the creator of the material dimensions we are all familiar with.

There are three spiritual forces in the earth. The Spirit of God, the spirit of man (as is noted in Genesis 2:7), and the spirit of Satan, who is in opposition to God, also alluded to in Genesis 3.

The first three chapters of Genesis describe the three moving forces that dominate the rest of history. All three spirits are in the realm of the fourth dimension, so naturally spirit can hover over the material third dimension and exercise creative powers. Of course, the human spirit and the spirit of the devil have definite limitations in exercising their fourth dimensional creative influence on the physical world. But God's spirit has no limitations.

As I continued to ponder these things, the Holy Spirit continued to give me the answer to my question. The Holy Spirit said, "My son, man still does not realize the spiritual power that I have given to him. Did I not want him to rule his environment?"

"Yes," I said, realizing what God was referring to. Man was originally told to name the other creatures that God had created. He was given the ability to cultivate the earth and grow his own food. He was to have dominion. When man fell, he still had a spirit, but his ability to communicate with God was lost. False prophets had power in the realm of the spirit because they had come to realize their potential. Christians had the greater power if they would only realize the power of the Holy Spirit that had been given to them.

Now the picture became very clear. Instead of fearing those who exercise spiritual powers motivated by Satan, we were to use the power of God, which is greater, to bring glory and honor to the Living God.

What about those who use their human powers? Human power is manifested when man realizes his natural ability (as a descendant of Adam). Man's power is limited, but the individual eventually will be drawn into the camp of Satan unless he yields to God.

The important thing I had to teach my church members was that the power in us is greater than any power that is in the world (1 John 4:4). As I shared these things with my people, the confusion vanished and a new era of understanding dawned upon us. Although this understanding came to me many years ago, I have continued to learn how to become more comfortable living in the fourth dimension. This does not mean that I have stopped living in the material world, but it does mean that I am becoming more aware of the greater sphere of spiritual existence we have as Christians.

What is man?

What is man? This important question is asked by David in a poetic way in Psalm 8. This psalm was sung by David during the festival of Israel commemorating the grape harvest. Gittith,* in its Hebrew root, means winepress. There are two other psalms sung near the winepress and they are also joyous and commemorative of the glory and excellency of God (Pss. 81, 84). Psalm 8 was written at night when all the stars were shining and David could appreciate the magnitude of God's creation. When David looked up at the greatness of God's creation, he realized the smallness of man and the futility of his pride.

Man is insignificant if you only consider his physical size. In comparison to the vastness of the earth, he is only a speck. Then, when you become aware of the solar system in which our earth is located, man becomes even less significant. Finally, being cognizant of the fact that one visible star can be millions of times larger than our own solar system, man becomes by comparison totally insignificant. Yet David's question must be completed: "What is man that thou art mindful of him?"

What gives man dignity is the fact that the Creator of our vast universe has chosen to center His attention on him, to the degree that God became man in Jesus Christ in order to save him. Man is not only dignified by God's attention and visitation, but he is also dignified by His high calling: "You have made him to have dominion

---

* Gittith is in the title of Psalm 8 and describes the location the Psalm was sung in.

over the works of Your hands; You have put all things under his feet" (Ps. 8, NKJV).

Man's blessed calling becomes through sin his curse in that his potentiality for dominion causes his aggression. Instead of desiring to rule God's creation, which was originally placed under his dominion, he has historically endeavored to rule other men. This is only one aspect of man's enigmatic nature. He has the ability both to ascend to the heights and descend to the depths. He is capable of the best and worst. He was created for so much, but settles for so little.

Yet, whether a saint or sinner, man was still created in the image of God. According to Genesis 1:26, man did not evolve from a lower form of life; he was created by God as man. He was also made in the image of God in that He placed His breath into him, causing him to be more than a material being. This is in sharp contrast to modern thought concerning man.

Our young people are taught in our schools that man evolved from a lower form of life. This could be one of the causes of man's present decline in morality and lifestyle. However, this notion is not new.

J.B. deMonet Lamarck, a well-known French naturalist of the nineteenth century, adopted a theory that all living things developed from simple germs that were placed on this earth by God, the one who created the universe. All living creatures became alive by developing cells capable of being stimulated by a force such as heat or electricity. Lamarck also stated that living things adopted new organs as the need arose through the process of selectivity. Lamarck published his work in 1809, the very year that Charles Darwin was born.

How could an unintelligent cell develop by itself and adopt to circumstances beyond its control? To someone studying these theories with the same critical standards men have studied the Bible's account of man's creation, he would have to exercise more faith in believing the former than the latter.

Although present theories have disputed Darwin, they have simply added another dimension to man's attempt to rid himself from a dependence upon a divine being in order to explain his origin. Modern man seemingly solves the dilemma of natural selection simply by adding time. If this is not possible in a comparatively short period of time, then it might be possible in a much longer period of time. Natural selection might even be possible in a period of time such as millions or billions of years.

The Biblical View

God elevates man from mere matter. This is why cultures that have accepted the biblical view of man have a respect for life and the individual. Biblical Christianity shows that man is more than what he seems to be. He is made in the image of God.

Man is made in the image of God in that he is a trinity: body, soul and spirit.

1. *Body*

Man was first created a physical being. God created him physically before He breathed into him the breath of life (Gen. 2:7). After his sin, man was told by God, ". . . Dust thou art, and unto dust shalt thou return" (Gen. 3:19, KJV). Therefore, man has a temporary body which dies and decays. Strangely, that part of man which is only temporary receives his most attention.

There are eight aspects of the Body, according to Scripture:

a. The body houses the soul and spirit (Dan. 7:15).
b. It is affected by the soul based upon what it sees (Matt. 6:22, 23).
c. It can be made alive by the Holy Spirit (divine health) (Romans 8:10).
d. It becomes the temple of the Holy Spirit at conversion (1 Cor. 6:19).
e. It is to be taken care of and not neglected (Col. 2:23).
f. It is strongly affected by our spoken words (James 3).

g. It is the chief symbol of the church (Eph. 4:12, 16).

h. It shall be transformed at the resurrection (1 Cor. 15:14).

2. *Soul*

The Old Testament makes a clear distinction between the soul and the body. In Eccles. 12:7, it is said, "Then shall the dust return to the earth as it was, and the spirit shall return unto God who gave it." In the New Testament, Jesus makes a clear distinction: "Fear not them which kill the body, but are not able to kill the soul: but rather fear him which is able to destroy both soul and body in hell" (Matt. 10:28, KJV). The soul and the body are so closely linked in our vital functions that often it is difficult to differentiate between the two.

The soul controls our will and desires and has a strong influence over the body. I have heard doctors tell me that often it is the person with the will to live that will survive a difficult operation. Since the soul also has what is referred to as the mind, there are many effects which the mind produces upon the physical body. For example, the mind sees, using the physical organs of the eyes. The mind hears, using the physical organs of the ears. The mind senses, using the body's ability to feel.

The soul also comprises that which we call emotions. Joy, shame and happiness are all emotions which also have an effect on the body. For example, if a person is embarrassed, he might blush, a physical manifestation of an emotional reaction. If a person becomes angry, it might cause him to have unusual strength in his muscles or cause his heart to beat much more quickly.

The soul also contains what we call desires. What a person desires often motivates his activities and physical nature. We have all heard of people that have trained their bodies to perform unusual athletic feats. This was done because of an unusual desire which drove the body to excellence.

The soul also comprises what a man calls his intellect and his taste. The soul is man's self; it is his conscious being. When we refer to someone, we are referring to more than his body, we are referring to the person. When we marry, we begin to develop a greater attraction for the person with whom we have a relationship than for the person's body. Although the body might cause intitial interest, the person will shine through their physical appearance. It is that person which is the soul of man.

3. *Spirit*

In understanding man's spirit nature, we come into a sphere of much controversy among theologians. Charles Hodge, in his *Systematic Theology*, states, "This doctrine of a threefold constitution of man being adopted by Plato, was introduced partially into the early Church, but soon came to be regarded as dangerous, if not heretical. Its being held by the Gnostics that the 'Pneuma' in man was a part of the divine essence, and incapable of sin; and by Apollinarians that Christ had only a human 'soma' and 'psucha,' but not a human 'pneuma.' The Church rejected the doctrine that the 'psucha' and the 'pneuma' were distinct substances, since upon it those heresies were founded. In later times the SemiPelagians taught that the soul and body, but not the spirit in man, were the subjects of original sin. All Protestants, Lutheran and Reformed, were, therefore, the more zealous in maintaining that the soul and spirit, 'psucha' and 'pneuma,' are one and the same substance and essence. And this, as before remarked, has been the common doctrine of the church."*

Hodge holds to the dichotomy of man and rejects the trichotomy of man. In other words, man is made up of only soul and body; not body, soul and spirit. Berkhof, in his *Systematic Theology* agrees with Hodge.

"The Teaching of Scripture as to the Constituent Elements of Human Nature. The prevailing representation of the nature of man in Scripture is clearly dichotomic. On the one hand the Bible teaches us to view the nature of man as a unity, and not as a duality, consisting of two different elements, each of which move along parallel lines but do not really unite to form

---

* *Systematic Theology,* part 2, page 51. Eerdmans Publishing.

a single organism. The idea of a mere parallelism between the two elements of human nature, found in Greek philosophy and also in the works of later philosophers, is entirely foreign to Scripture."*

These scholars point to Gen. 2:7 where there is no mention made of a spirit being created by God. However, we must remember that it is told in chapter 3 that man sinned and that the result of his sin would be death. If man died, then what died? Obviously he continued to live with a body and consciousness, so what died was his spirit. Also in 1 Thes. 5:23, we can see that Paul is making a distinction: "Now may the God of peace Himself sanctify you completely; and may your whole spirit, soul, and body be preserved blameless at the coming of our Lord Jesus Christ."

The writer of Hebrews also makes a distinction: "For the Word of God is living, and active and sharper than any two-edged sword, and piercing even to the dividing of soul and spirit, of both joints and marrow, and quick to discern the thoughts and intents of the heart" (Heb. 4:12, NKJV).

Paul places Adam and Christ in juxtaposition and shows the former bringing death to man and the latter bringing life (Rom. 5:17, 19; 1 Cor. 15:22). And especially in 1 Cor. 15:45, "And so it is written, The first man, Adam, was made a living soul; the last Adam was

---

* *Systematic Theology,* part 2, section 2, page 192. Eerdmans Publishing.

made a quickening Spirit." In the verse just quoted, Paul again divides soul and spirit. Adam was made a soul, through his sin, but through Christ's sinless nature, we are able to be made alive by His life-giving spirit.

Although it is not my desire to solve the theological disagreement which has lasted for the entire history of the church in this book, I believe the issue does not warrant a charge of heresy in either camp. Perhaps, what Paul refers to as spirit is a heightened aspect of the redeemed soul. Yet what remains certain is that man becomes different after the new birth. His spirit is made alive by the Holy Spirit and he is brought into a new dimension of spiritual experience with which he must become familiar. The spirit is that part of man that is made alive by Christ so that he might have vital union and communication with his Creator.

Five Aspects of Our Spirits

1. God wants to direct our lives, by His Spirit (Romans 8:14).

2. Man in his natural state is incapable of understanding spiritual reality. In fact, spiritual things seem foolish to him (1 Cor. 2:14).

3. Spiritual men are to differentiate between those things that are of God and those things which are of this world or of Satan, because he has developed his spiritual senses (1 Cor. 2:15).

4. Only those who have developed their spiritual senses are capable of understanding mature things (Heb. 5:14).

5. Spiritual people are ones that are not destroyers but ones who are restorers of those who have fallen (Gal. 6:1).

As I have previously indicated, the lesser is always contained in the greater. However, there should be no confusion. God desires that we keep in mind that we are not three people vying for power. We were not created to be divided too distinctly. We are one person; however, we have different functions within our one person that must be understood if we are to grow and develop as whole men.

Our bodies are important. We are commanded not to neglect them. The Christian should therefore be concerned about his health by eating properly, exercising and adopting the proper habits. What is often the case is that people have a tendency to over-emphasize one aspect of their nature above the others. A man who is more intellectually oriented should not feel that his body is unimportant. A spiritual person should not neglect his intellectual or physical condition. In all things there must be a balance. The greater does not mean to detract from the lesser; the greater includes the lesser.

Visions and Dreams:
The Instruments of the Fourth Dimension

If a man understands what he is, he will desire to know how he can grow in his fourth-dimensional capabilities. If the Holy Spirit has come to lead us and guide us into all truth, how does He operate?

The age of the Holy Spirit began on the day of Pentecost. Peter preached his first message the day that the Holy Spirit came in clear manifestation. His text was from Joel 2: "And it shall come to pass in the last days, saith God, I will pour out of my Spirit upon all flesh; and your sons and your daughters shall prophesy, and your young men shall see visions, and your old men shall dream dreams" (Acts 2:17, KJV).

Dreams and visions are very similar in nature. Young men have a tendency to envision the future; old men naturally dream about the past. However, both dreams and visions work within the framework of the imagination.

Before we can understand how visions and dreams operate, we should understand something about the framework within which they operate: the imagination.

The Imagination: the Soul of the Vision and Dream

In 2 Cor. 10, Paul tells us that we are to walk in the Holy Spirit and not in the flesh. The King James Version uses the word "imagination" in the fifth verse. However, the word could be better translated "reasonings" or "logic." Paul does not mean that we should not reason, but he does tell us not to rely on our natural logic that has not been sanctified by the Holy Spirit. Our problems are greater than just natural ones and the solutions must be found by using our spiritual minds. "For the weapons of our warfare are not carnal but mighty in God for pulling down strongholds, casting down arguments and every high thing that exalts itself against the knowledge of God, bringing every thought into captivity to the obedience of Christ" (2 Cor. 10:4-5, NKJV).

Paul uses military language when referring to the realm of the imagination. The unregenerated mind uses natural reason which cannot understand spiritual things. Paul refers to these natural reasonings as strongholds of fortifications which the spiritual mind must bring down in order for the Christian to live victoriously.

When the Bible refers to the heart, it is referring to the area of our soul which comprises the imagination. Jesus said, "Let not your heart be troubled"(John 14:1, NKJV). There are seven areas which Jesus revealed were problems in the heart:

1. The heart can be hardened to spiritual reality (Mark 6:52).

2. The heart can be blind, incapable of seeing what would be obvious to the spiritual person (John 12:40).

3. The heart is where sin begins (Matt. 15:19).

4. Words spoken are first conceived in the heart (Matt. 12:34).

5. Satan operates his tempting powers in the heart (John 13:2).

6. Doubts begin in the heart (Mark 11:23).

7. Sorrow and trouble work within the heart (John 14:1, 16:6).

Therefore, Paul's teaching the Corinthian Christians to guard their hearts was based on the clear emphasis which Christ gave to this important part of the soul.

I liken the heart of man to a painter's canvas. What a man dreams and envisions is the paint. If the Christian takes the brush of faith and begins to paint on the canvas of his heart the pictures that God has revealed to him, those revelations become reality.

The Unconscious Mind

What is referred to as the subconscious is really the unconscious mind. The unconscious mind is the motivational force that causes men to act or to behave without conscious perception. I have noticed a number of books on this subject in recent years.

Carl Gustav Jung, the son of a clergyman and a student of Sigmund Freud, developed the field of psychology known as analytical psychology as a reaction to Freud's psychoanalysis. In his view, man was not only motivated by conscious thought and reasoning, but also by his unconscious mind. He broke down the unconscious into two categories: 1. the personal factor or one's individual unconscious; 2. the collective factor or one's collective unconscious that is inherited from one's ancestors.

There developed a sociological belief that man's collective unconscious was inherently good. Society's rules were thought to tend to inhibit man. Anthropologists, artists and philosophers began traveling to primitive cultures searching for the goodness and simplicity in man which had not been spoiled by the prohibitions of Western culture.

The belief in man's inherent goodness is in direct contradiction to Scripture. "The heart is deceitful above all things, and desperately wicked; Who can know it? I, the Lord, search the heart, I test the mind, even to give every man according to his ways, and according to the fruit of his doings" (Jer. 17:9-10, NKJV).

God reveals to man in Jer. 3 things about his heart: (1) The heart is not inherently good, but inherently evil. This is because of sin; (2) Man is not naturally capable of understanding his own heart. Only the Lord knows a man's heart and is capable of revealing it to him; (3) A man's actions will reveal his heart.

If our actions and accomplishments result from a motivating force that is beyond our conscious perception, then should not the Holy Spirit choose to work within this realm in order to sanctify it and cause it to motivate us to do God's will?

The Ability to See and Dream

The Holy Spirit is pictured by Peter at the day of Pentecost as a river. God had promised to pour this river into humanity irrespective of social standing, gender, or age. Joel prophesied that the moderate former rain and the stronger latter, or harvest, rain would both fall at once in "the day of the Lord." The torrents of God's Holy Spirit forming a spiritual river would fill every believer and bring forth spiritual fruit.

When the final day of the first fruits, (first harvest) festival arrived, the Holy Spirit descended in a forceful manner. It must be remembered that the Pentecost feast (fifty days after the wave offering of the Passover festival) was a feast of anticipation. If there was a good grain harvest, then the fruit harvest, celebrated as the Feast of Tabernacles, would also be good.

The Church was born within the festival of anticipation. The anticipation will be culminated at the Second Coming of Jesus Christ. By that time, the Church will have accomplished her divine purpose of bringing the gospel of Jesus Christ to every creature. The success of the Church is assured because the Holy Spirit has empowered her with supernatural ability.

The Holy Spirit came on the day of Pentecost not only to cause men to be able to prophesy (speak forth the Word of God), but also to give the ability to have visions and dreams.

In the Old Testament we often see God giving visions

and dreams concerning future events. In fact, Samuel was called a seer (1 Sam. 9:9). Daniel was able to see from Babylon the development of successive kingdoms and looked into the Church age and beyond. Ezekiel could see beyond his land into a foreign land.

This phenomenon was not limited to the Old Testament. In the New Testament, Ananias, Paul and even a Roman, Cornelius, had prophetic visions and dreamed dreams.

This does not necessarily mean that we should all remain in ecstatic states. However, it does mean that we are to participate in God fulfilling His will in our lives by first envisioning His purpose and then filling our imagination with it through dreaming.

Consequently, the believer should not be limited to the three-dimension plane, but should go beyond that into the fourth-dimensional plane of reality. We should live in the Spirit. We should guard our minds from all negative and foolish thinking. This keeps the canvas clean for the artwork of the Holy Spirit to be painted on our imaginations. Creativity, perception, intelligence, and spiritual motivation will be by-products of an imagination which has been activated by the Holy Spirit.

"For as he thinks in his heart, so is he" (Prov. 23:7, NKJV). There is no question in my mind that we become what we think, either for good or for evil. Television has had a great effect upon our present society.

The Fourth Dimension

Whenever I hear television people say that they don't affect society but they only mirror society, I then ask myself, "Why do corporations spend so much money on commercials?" The violence and amoral sexual activity depicted on television are responsible for much of the decay we see in society today.

Satan is out to destroy men's minds so that man will not be able to accomplish his purpose in this world. Pornographic movies and magazines cause minds to treat sex as an animalistic activity, thereby destroying man's dignity and self-image. Why? Because we eventually become what we dwell upon.

This is the reason God is so concerned with what we think. "Finally, brethren, whatever things are true, whatever things are noble, whatever things are just, . . . whatever things are of good report, if there is any virtue and if there is anything praiseworthy—meditate on these things" (Phil. 4:8, NKJV).

Becoming what we think is not only true for those who are motivated towards negative thinking, but also those who are desirous of doing the will of God. If you dwell on what God has destined for you to become, you will become just that. Therefore, I ask my people never to allow negative thoughts to dwell in their minds but to think positive things. A businessman will not succeed if he dwells on failure. If a person in my church fails, I tell him, "You are not a failure because you failed. You are only a failure if you don't try again.

Fill your mind with success and you will become successful."

Results of Fourth-Dimensional Thinking

Your success or failure depends upon your fourth-dimensional thinking: visions and dreams. We see this principle in operation from the very beginning of Scripture.

What caused Eve to eat the forbidden fruit? Her mind knew what God had said. She was aware of the consequences of her actions. But, Paul said, she was deceived. How was Eve deceived? The serpent asked Eve to look at the forbidden tree. When her eyes focused on the tree she began to admire it. Her imagination began to work; she wondered what it would be like to eat the fruit and be released from her innocence. She would never have been deceived if she had not allowed her imagination to begin to work upon an act of disobedience to God. Her failure came as a result of using her fourth-dimensional thinking in the wrong way.

Sodom was a place of extreme sin and perversion. God decided to destroy the city, but determined that Lot and his family would be spared. Living in the midst of Sodom's society must have had a powerfully adverse effect upon Lot's family. Therefore, God told them to leave and not look back. Although she had been warned not to do so, Lot's wife looked back at Sodom and became a pillar of salt. While this was happening, Abram was on a mountain top seeing the same thing. Why was Abram able to look and Lot's wife was not?

Her heart had been affected by Sodom's lifestyle. When she looked back at the wicked city, her imagination longed for what she had left behind. Abram had not contaminated himself with the sinful lifestyle God was destroying; therefore he was free from judgment.

We are not told in Gen. 19 how long she looked at Sodom before she became a pillar of salt; but she looked long enough to let her imaginative powers fill her heart with the remorse for what she was leaving behind, thereby becoming a partaker of the destroyed city's judgment. Lot's wife failed by misusing her fourth-dimensional thinking.

Abraham the Dreamer

God's testimony to Abraham's faith in Hebrews 11 is quite revealing. He was able to leave Ur of the Chaldees, the center of civilization, and travel to a place that had not been shown him. I can imagine that Abraham's first test was his conversation with Sarah. "We are leaving!" Abraham said to his wife.

"Where are we going, dear?" Sarah answered.

"I don't know, just pack," Abraham said.

"How are we to know when we get there if we don't know where we are going? What has gotten into you,

Abe? Why are we leaving?" she asked, thinking that Abraham had succumbed to too much heat.

"God told me, so let's go!" Abraham responded, hoping that God would reveal the place he was going once he got there.

When Abraham came out of Egypt and Lot left him, he was commanded to look north and south, east and west of Canaan. All the real estate that he could see would be his. He could only possess what he could see. God only gave to Abraham what his eyes projected upon his imagination. His vision became his boundary line.

We never grow beyond our vision. Our experience will always be limited by what our vision sees. We learn this important spiritual lesson from Abraham.

All who are in Christ are heirs of the promise made to our spiritual father Abraham. Therefore, the innumerable number of God's children who have dwelled upon this earth from the time of Isaac till today are all the children of Abraham, whether they are of the natural or spiritual branch (Jew or Gentile). How did a one-hundred-year-old man become the father of so many? He used fourth-dimensional thinking. He was full of visions and dreams. He learned to incubate in faith.

It took twenty-five years for God's promise to come to pass, but it did come to pass. Abraham took several detours from the road of faith, but those detours are not mentioned in the letter to the Hebrews. Abraham's failures should cause all of us to believe that we are all capable of accomplishing the will of God to its fullest. His imperfection should encourage us to know that God doesn't use perfect people in accomplishing His perfect will.

God's commandment to Abraham was threefold: 1. He was to see the land (Gen. 13:14-16); 2. Abraham was told to look up to the stars. He was asked to number them. They represented his spiritual children (Gen. 15:53); 3. His name was changed from Abram to Abraham, which means "father of a great multitude."

1. By looking out in every direction, he filled his imagination in a concrete way with God's promise. He was not told to close his eyes when God spoke to him. He was told to look at something concrete and substantive. So often, when we are believing for something from God, we tend to neglect the role God expects us to play in the fulfillment of His promise. We are not to be idle or passive. God expects our faith to have form and substance. The Holy Spirit incubated the earth when it was without form and substance into a habitable planet. If the Holy Spirit had not incubated the earth into its present form, our earth would be like the rest of the planets in our solar system. So God expects us also to be active in the incubation of our faith by visualizing the final results of His promise.

My church has not grown to its present membership of 275,000 people because I am the most gifted pastor in the world. No. It has grown to its present size because I have followed Abraham's principle of visualization. In 1984, I see my church having half a million members. I can count them. I can see their faces in my heart. By 1985, I see our television program being aired throughout all of Korea, Japan and our English version in the United States and Canada. I see it. I have maps of these countries in my office and I have a clear vision of the transmitters beaming the programs.

2. When God focused Abraham's attention on his future seed, he was told to look at the stars. God wanted the sensitive film of his heart to capture not only the magnitude of the picture, but the lens of his eye was to capture each individual star in its individual beauty. Every one of his children were to be important to him, therefore, he was told to try to number each of them.

Each one of our children are different in their looks and personality. I have three boys. They are all different. I don't look out over the dinner table and see one picture depicting my children. I see each child individually.

I am sure that when Abraham went home at night, he could not get the stars out of his mind; his imagination was already filled with God's promise. His fourth-dimensional power began its work which resulted in a hundred-year-old man being able to naturally make his wife pregnant. This was because the fourth-dimensional vision dominated the third-dimensional physical circumstances.

3. God changed Abram's name to Abraham. His self-image had to be changed. He had to start calling himself "father of many." His family, friends and workers had to change their thinking. They could no longer refer to him in the way they had in the past. Every time he heard his name, he was reminded of God's promise.

We cannot keep God's promise to us a secret from others. We must begin to speak as if the promise had already come to pass. "God calls those things which are not as if they were." We must follow His example. God has to deliver us from the fear of what others will think. We have to let our words agree with our vision.

But the miracle had to take place in Sarah as well. At first she laughed when she heard that God would make her a mother at the age of ninety. However, she began to visualize the return of her youth. She dwelt upon the promise of God and soon a physical change began to take place in her. Even king Abimelech found the old woman so attractive that he tried to take her as his concubine. If a woman begins to think of herself as attractive, she can be. Not only will physical changes take place, but her self-image will change and she will begin to take better care of herself and start to dress as an attractive person.

We must remember that the birth of Isaac was only a miracle in that two elderly people were physically able to conceive. God did not just hand them a baby from the sky. Both Abraham and Sarah participated in the fulfillment of God's promise. They allowed the canvas of their hearts to be painted with the artwork of faith in God's Word.

"For we are His workmanship, created in Christ Jesus for good works, which God prepared beforehand that we should walk in them" (Eph. 2:10, NKJV). The Greek word translated workmanship is the word *poema,* from which we get the English word poem. It literally means "a work of art." God created us as a work of art in Christ with the purpose of accomplishing His work in the earth. Although we may have personality flaws, God sees us as complete in Christ. "For in Him dwells all the fullness of the Godhead bodily; and you are complete in Him, who is the head of all principality and power" (Col. 2:9, 10, NKJV). If God has painted a picture of us in Christ as complete and has openly communicated it to us through the Apostle Paul, should we not follow His example?

Isaac is not a Dreamer

As we continue to follow the family of faith, we notice that the life of Isaac was unlike the life of Abraham. The "son of promise" was not a dreamer like his father. We don't see the example of faith in Isaac to the degree that was evident in his father. Therefore, we don't see the works of faith in action in his life. Isaac lived in his father's visions and dreams. He never allowed the Holy Spirit to create the same relationship with God that his father possessed.

Jacob the Dreamer

Isaac had two sons, Jacob and Esau. Esau was a man's man; he was interested in hunting. Being strong and self-reliant, he was not too interested in the spiritual inheritance that belonged to him as the firstborn son. Jacob, which means "supplanter," was a man who was close to his mother and who enjoyed staying home. He was a natural deceiver. Most of us would have nothing to do with him, especially in business. Yet Jacob had one quality which distinguished him from his brother. He was a dreamer.

Having deceived his brother and later his father, Jacob had to leave home, fleeing for his life. He journeyed to a relative's farm. Jacob learned something from his experience with Laban: deceivers get deceived.

Jacob worked for seven years for the right to marry Rachel, Laban's younger daughter. However, Laban wanted his older daughter, Leah, married first. So, after the wedding party, Laban exchanged daughters. Jacob, who was guilty of misrepresentation, became victim of the same sin himself.

Jacob had to work another seven years for the wife he originally wanted. Therefore, Jacob ended up with two wives. However, God chose to bring forth Christ through the offspring of the first wife, Leah, whose fourth son was Judah, (a name which means "praise").

Laban had been greatly blessed because of Jacob's service. It was obvious to him that Jacob had something unusual, something which had to come from God. Yet Jacob desired to leave and build his own household. In order for him to leave, he needed means to provide for his wives and children. So he devised a scheme whereby he could become a rich man.

He told Laban that he would pass through his large flock and remove all of the speckled and spotted sheep, all of the brown lambs and all of the spotted and speckled goats. These were obviously of less value than the pure white ones. He then assured Laban that if ever there were found pure sheep, lambs and goats in his flocks, then they should be considered stolen.

Laban did not believe that Jacob could possibly be serious. He said to Jacob, "Oh, that it were according to your word!" So Laban took all of the spotted and speckled flocks and told his children to bring them about three-days journey away from where Jacob was living. This left Jacob with nothing. The prospects were dim that Jacob would ever have anything because it was unlikely that pure sheep and goats would ever conceive hybrid, colored flocks. Laban thought that he could keep Jacob working for free forever. However, Jacob had learned how to have visions and dreams.

Jacob had begun to dream at Bethel, where he had built his first altar to the God of Abraham. Learning from his grandfather's experience, and discovering that his trickery would not accomplish his divine calling, he turned to God. God showed him how to create something from nothing; by taking impossibility and making it opportunity.

Jacob, being in charge of Laban's flock, began to dream spotted and speckled as he viewed the pure flock. He used spotted and speckled polls to concentrate his vision as the pure flocks were watering.

In time, the pure flocks began to conceive according to Jacob's dream. It was beyond Laban's comprehension how the miracle took place. But when explaining to his family why he had to leave, Jacob revealed his secret, "And it happened, at the time when the flocks conceived, that I lifted my eyes and saw in a dream, and behold, the rams which leaped upon the flocks were streaked, speckled, and grayspotted" (Gen. 31:10).

It was through using his fourth-dimensional ability (visions and dreams) that Jacob was able to leave Laban with almost his entire flock. Jacob heard the Word and filled his imagination with the promise. Laban's treachery only made the miracle even more spectacular. For Laban changed his wages ten times during the time Jacob had agreed to work. Yet when the blessing of God is upon you, no obstacle can stand in the way of success.

Joseph the Dreamer

Jacob had twelve sons, but only one of them (Joseph) learned the secret to success. Having returned to the land of his fathers, Jacob (now called Israel) put Joseph in charge of his flocks. Joseph was his father's favorite son because he was the son of his old age. Seeing the open favoritism, the other brothers became extremely jealous. Their hostility became more acute when, at the age of seventeen, Joseph began to dream.

"Please hear this dream," Joseph told his brothers. "There we were, binding sheaves in the field. Then behold, my sheaf arose and also stood upright; and indeed your sheaves stood all around and bowed down to my sheaf." The circumstances which could have brought about the fulfillment of the dream became even more impossible when Joseph was sold into slavery in Egypt. As the circumstances became more desperate, Joseph's dreams became more important in his life. Finally, the dream came to pass when Joseph became prime minister of Egypt. His famine-stricken family, which had come to Egypt for food, all bowed down to him.

God is called the God of Abraham, Isaac and Jacob.

God is linked to those who follow His example of incubating results through visions and dreams.

No Bankruptcies

The past few years have been difficult for our business community in Korea. We have suffered a very severe recession. Interest rates have been high and inflation has cut deeply into our people's purchasing power. Yet, more than in times of prosperity, we see God's principles at work during hard times.

Through continually teaching my people the principles of success found in the Scriptures, we have seen no bankruptcies in our church. Our income has remained constant and we have embarked on the largest building program in our church's history. What has been the key to our practical success in business? We have taught our people how to use their fourth-dimensional powers. They visualize success. We do not dwell on negative thinking, but speak positive words motivated by positive thinking. Since we do not have the same tax structure in our country as is enjoyed by the church in other countries, our people have learned how to tithe and give sacrificially without tax breaks. What I am sharing in this book is practical and can be used by any believer anywhere in the world. It is part of the manifold wisdom of God that He has taken a man from a small country which is part of the developing world to build the largest church on this earth. No one could have predicted it, but through incubation we have seen God take our small gifts and use them to influence Korea and the world.

God can do the same thing through you!

Incubating Your Healing

On Christmas Eve several years ago, I received an urgent phone call from a medical doctor whom I knew. "Pastor Cho, please come down to the hospital! One of your church members has been in a terrible accident and we don't expect him to last the night," the doctor said. Later I found out that this young man had just left work and was heading home to his family. Since it was Christmas Eve, he had bought his wife a special Christmas present and was preoccupied with the thought of how pleased with it she would be. He never saw the taxi that was speeding in his direction. Since it was late at night there were no witnesses. At that time, in Korea, if an automobile would strike a pedestrian, he was fined $2,500 and that was all. However, if the pedestrian lived, then the driver was responsible for all of the expenses the victim incurred until his recovery. So the driver of the cab dragged him into the back seat and began driving around the city, hoping that he would die.

After several hours, someone noticed the injured man in the back seat and called the police.

The man was rushed to the hospital, and found to be very close to death. His condition was aggravated by the fact that his intestinal tract was ripped open and dirt had caused an infection.

As I arrived at the hospital, I was told by the doctor that his condition was worsening and that he was unconscious. Yet I walked into the room knowing that circumstances don't dictate to God what He is not able to accomplish. There are no such things as easy or difficult miracles. To God, the parting of the Red Sea is no more difficult than healing someone's headache.

I went by the man's bed and prayed out loud: "Dear Lord, allow this brother to regain his consciousness for just five minutes." As I was praying, I opened my eyes and noticed that he was looking right at me. I could see the terror in his eyes as he pictured himself dying. What would happen to his wife? Who would take care of his children? These were the thoughts that must have been running through his mind.

Knowing that God had answered my prayer by giving him back his consciousness, and realizing that he would only have five minutes to hear what I had to say, I began to speak to him.

"I know what you are thinking," I said. "You are already envisioning death. But God wants you to participate in the miracle that is going to take place. The reason you have regained your consciousness is that God wants to use your fourth-dimensional power and begin to paint a new picture upon the canvas of your heart."

As I spoke these words, I could hear the nurse laughing quietly in the background. But this was no time to be self-conscious. This man was dying and I had to obey what the Holy Spirit was telling me to do. Therefore, ignoring the nurse, I continued. "I want you to start painting a new picture of yourself in your imagination. You are on your way home and no accident has taken place. You knock on the door and your lovely wife answers. She looks very pretty. On Christmas Day she opens up her present and you feel so proud you have such good taste. The next morning you wake up and have a good breakfast with your family. In other words, you are erasing death from your mind and you're painting a new picture of happiness.

"Do you have the picture? Is it clear?" I asked, hoping that he would be able to hear and understand the full implication of what I was saying. I could see his eyes light up for the first time.

I continued, "You leave the praying to me! I will pray in faith and you agree with me! Just use your ability to dream and see visions of your health and happiness!"

When I prayed, I could feel the Holy Spirit very powerfully in the room. The nurse then said, "Pastor, I'm sorry to interrupt your prayer, but it has gotten very warm in this room. Don't you think so? Perhaps I'll open the window and let in some fresh air."

I knew that the room temperature had not changed and it was cold outside on this December night. Yet the nurse was sensing something that she could not understand. That something was God's power at work.

I continued praying, this time laying my hands on the bed. The bed began to shake. God was performing a miracle for His glory. Within a few days, the man returned to his wife and family, having been completely healed by the power of God.

He then shared with me how when I asked him to change his imagination from death to life, he began to sense a deep peace come over his body. He was no longer asking God to live, he began praising God because he was sure God was going to heal him.

The man is now in the chemical business and is very successful. Whenever I notice him in church, (he comes every Sunday but it's hard for me to see everyone), I remember the story and I praise God.

When the blind man approached Jesus, he knew that he was blind. However, Jesus asked him, "What do you want me to do for you?" Jesus wanted the man to be specific and as he confessed that he knew Christ could give him back his sight, he started to receive a new vision of himself. His faith began to rise and he could imagine himself able to see, able to work, and possibly able to have a regular life, instead of being a beggar. Jesus said to him, "Your faith has made you whole." The blind man was healed.

It Is God's Desire to Give Prosperity and Health

"Beloved, I pray that you may prosper in all things and be in health, just *as your soul prospers*"(3 John 2, NKJV). Our souls' condition will affect the condition of our whole body. God desires for all Christians to prosper in body, soul and spirit. According to John, the key to prosperity is the soul.

A Healthy Soul Life

It is not God's will for us to have an unhealthy soul. He wants our minds clear to accomplish His will. He wants our desires to be pure so that we will use our desires in the incubation process. He wants our emotions healthy so we don't become depressed and discouraged. As we guard our hearts, we will find a healthy soul capable of hearing what the Holy Spirit speaks to our spirits and able to put into action our fourth-dimensional capabilities.

God's Word Is Not Limited

The great difference between people is the degree with which they are able to use their fourth-dimensional ability. The material world is governed by arguments and reason. We use reason, but we are able to go one step further. We have the Holy Spirit, who has invaded this three-dimensional plane of reality and is desirous of guiding us into a new plane.

The Word of God is not limited to the three-dimensional plane. Paul said he was not ashamed of the gospel of Jesus Christ because it was the power of God. He used reason in order to explain the great mysteries of the Kingdom of God. But Paul was not limited to reason. He told the Corinthians that he came to them in the demonstration of the spirit and power. Therefore, their faith would not be limited to natural wisdom but would transcend it.

The writer of the Letter to the Hebrews stated that the Word was sharp and powerful. It had the ability to not only reach the mind, but it could even penetrate the very intents of the heart.

Therefore, the Christian is equipped with the Word and the Holy Spirit. With these tools at his disposal, he can comfortably face any challenge and see the victory.

Satan's counterfeits are going to be increasingly manifested as the end draws near. There are going to be many claiming to be like Christ and will even manifest unusual power. But we should not be fooled by them nor fear them in any way. For as the Church draws to the end, she shall be equipped by the Holy Spirit with the grace to use the spiritual weapons at her disposal and see God's divine purpose accomplished in the earth.

The Devil's Counterfeit

As we enter into the closing era of the Church age, the Devil is unleashing his counterfeits as never before.

It is no wonder we are seeing an increasing number of false religions springing up in the very seed-bed of modern Christianity, Europe and America. As God's people are entering a new understanding of fourth-dimensional Christianity and are seeing God performing miracles in their lives, so also spurious religions are performing their own brands of miracles.

Moses experienced the same thing when he was called to deliver Israel from the bondage of Egypt. "The LORD spoke to Moses and Aaron, saying, 'When Pharaoh speaks to you, saying, "Show a miracle for yourselves," then you shall say to Aaron, "Take your rod and cast it before Pharaoh, and let it become a serpent." So Moses and Aaron went into Pharaoh and they did so, just as he LORD commanded. And Aaron cast down his rod before Pharaoh and before his servants, and it became a serpent. But Pharaoh also called the wise men and the sorcerers; so the magicians of Egypt, they also did like manner with their enchantments. For every man threw down his rod, and they became serpents. But Aaron's rod swallowed up their rods" (Exod. 7:8-12, NKJV).

One of the most deceitful false religions which is gaining popularity in the West is Zen Buddhism. In the past twenty years, many of the intellectual centers in Europe and America have increasingly turned to this religion which we in the East are increasingly discarding. Thomas Altizer has said, "Today, Buddhism is the religion that is most profoundly challenging Christianity (particularly in its Zen form). Contemplation is the highest of man's activity. For therein he can become God and therein can he become immortal . . . Genuine Christianity is the ultimate form of rebellion."[1]

While evangelical Christians are increasingly understanding how to use their imaginations by learning how to speak the language of the Holy Spirit (visions and dreams), the Zen Buddhists are increasing their activity in the West and are even affecting Christian centers of learning. As they teach people to look inside themselves and contemplate, they are producing counterfeit experiences, including miracles.

I have found it difficult to understand why Western intellectuals bypass Christianity and look to Oriental mysticism for spiritual fulfillment. As I travel throughout India and Japan, I see young European and American men and women in Oriental dress obviously searching for a spiritual experience to justify their existence. These people have abandoned their Christian heritage sociologically and psychologically and have turned to doctrines of devils that we have been delivered from in the East.

What has caused these sincere searchers for reality to look in Oriental temples for what is available in their local churches? Why has the Western church not been able to meet the need of its young intellectuals? These are questions that have caused me to concern myself with the Church in the West. As I have traveled throughout Europe and the Americas, I have discovered the problem. So many traditional churches have forgotten the vitality of Christianity and have become dead and sterile. This is why attendance in churches in many Western countries had dropped continually in the past twenty years, while churches in former mission fields have grown dramatically.

The Western Spiritual Void

Arnold Toynbee said: "Man has been a dazzling success in the field of intellect and 'knowhow,' but a dismal failure in the things of spirit."[2] Toynbee's *Civilization on Trial,* traces the decline of Western thinking from its spiritual origins in biblical Christianity. Western culture extracted from its spiritual roots in the gospel took many years to disintegrate into what it has become today. Therefore, the spiritual void created in the heart of Western man has become a fertile soil for the seeds of Eastern false religion.

Albert Schweitzer stated that without a moral factor or foundation, all human endeavors, scientific inventions, cultures, and civilization itself would be doomed to decline and corruption.[3] Schweitzer's understanding of modern man's spiritual dilemma caused him to conclude that Western man needed to return to his spiritual roots in Christianity.

European culture as we know it today was founded on the spiritual philosophy of Augustine. His *City of God* became the cornerstone from which the building of honesty, hard work and positive self-image became an integral part of Western society. Before his teachings reached northern Europe, the Germanic and Scandinavian people were nothing like they are today. Philip Schaff said, "In his passion, the old Scandinavian was sometimes worse than a beast. Gluttony and drunkenness he considered as accomplishments. In his energy, he was sometimes fiercer than a demon. Revenge was the noblest sentiment and passion of man; forgiveness was a sin. The battlefield reeking with blood and fire was the highest beauty the earth could show; patient and peaceful labor was an abomination. They slew the missionaries and burnt their schools and churches. After a contest of more than a century, it became apparent that Christianity would be victorious; the pagan heroes left the country in great swarms as if they were fleeing from some awful plague."[4]

The Church conquered with the most powerful force known to man, the gospel of Jesus Christ. After many centuries of spiritual decline, during which churches lost their moral strength, Europe experienced the Reformation. John Calvin, Martin Luther, and John Knox not only had a religious influence upon their societies, but their influence permeated society as a whole. Although the Reformers were not overly concerned with missions, it has to be understood that they were fighting for the mere survival of biblical Christianity. It is upon the sacrifice of the Reformers that the late eighteenth- and nineteeth-century missionary movement rested. Once the Church was strong in what it believed and had influenced its own society, she was ready to reach out to the ends of the world.

However, beginning with Friedrich Schleiermacher (1768-1834), known as the father of modern theology, the church in Europe began to retreat into its present humanistic theology. Instead of depending on the Word of God as the Reformers had done, Schleiermacher began his concept of religion by calling it "feeling of absolute dependence." Although traditional Christians largely ignored Schleiermacher, his theology was to have a profound influence on all subsequent theology.

Ritschl, Von Harnack and Kierkegaard continued to motivate theology, and in turn their societies, resulting in the spiritual void many traditional churches have experienced to this day.

Carl Gustav Jung observed that modern man has lost all the metaphysical certainties of his medieval brother and set up in their place the ideals of material security. But it takes more than ordinary doses of optimism. Even material security has gone by the boards for modern man has begun to see that every step in material progress only adds so much force to the threat of a more stupendous catastrophe. Science has destroyed even the refuge of the inner life. What was once a sheltering haven has become a place of terror. The rapid and worldwide progressive growth of interest in psychology shows modern man has turned his attention from material things to his own subjective process. Jung observed that many people in our society consider Freud more important than the Gospels.[5] It is this very aspect of man's thinking that has produced what Rousas Rushdoony calls "intellectual schizophrenia."

It is upon the cultural, spiritual, philosophical and religious bankruptcy of Western thinking that Zen has gained influence.

Where Did Zen Come From?

Zen had its origins in India. The story is told that when Buddha was teaching his disciples upon a mountain, a Brahma-Raja (a royal priest) came to him with a Lotus flower and asked him to preach Dharma (law and truth). Instead of teaching, the story goes, Buddha simply gazed at the flower in complete silence. Confused by the continued silence of Lord Buddha, the disciples wondered what the Master was doing. The only one that understood was Mahakasyapa, a trusted disciple. He simply smiled and nodded his head. It is said that the wisdom received that day was transmitted in silence through the leadership of twenty-eight Patriarchs, Buddha being the first. It was the twenty-eighth Patriarch, Bodhi-Dharma (A.D. 480-528), who came to China during the Liang Dynasty who became the founder of Zen Buddhism in China.

During the seventh century, the Zen School of Buddhism split into two sects. The one which was mainly practiced in Northern China known as the school of "gradual" enlightenment, only lasted one hundred years. The other sect, which believed in "instantaneous" enlightenment, continued to prosper and became the dominant Chinese religion.

Having reached Japan in the seventh century, the Japanese adopted Zen to its particular sociology. It became the religion of the military class, with its emphasis on rigor, self-discipline and contempt for death. However, by the thirteenth century, China began to lose interest in Zen, and turned to other forms of religion more in keeping with her own distinctive culture. My own country of Korea was influenced by Zen Buddhism which was brought to us by the Chinese.

What Is Zen?

Zen is not logical. In fact, as an iconoclastic mental process, Zen can be considered a non-religion. Zen seeks to draw man into himself to seek for nothingness or "the bottomless abyss." It seeks to "enlighten" man by causing him to bypass his natural reasoning and find an "ultimate essence of being."

If you ask a practitioner of Zen if it is a philosophy, he would say, "No. We teach ourselves; Zen only points the way."[6] Zen also claims not to be a religion, but a way to discover. It does not claim to be Buddhism, but the pinnacle of Buddhism. In essence, Zen tries to point man in the direction of himself. It rejects the concept of sin and salvation, and causes man to find reality through "self-hypnosis." To a Zen practitioner, "Form is Void and Void is Form." It leads man to seek for the nothingness in which he might find peace. The feeling of peace or "Enlightenment" is called *Wu.*

The Impact of Zen in the West

Zen has had a considerable impact in Europe and America. With the traditional churches becoming further alienated from Western society, the spiritual void created has to a large measure been filled by spurious religions such as Zen.

Alan Watts, formerly an Episcopal clergyman, was one of the leading advocates of Zen in the West. His statements concerning Christianity clearly validate the writings of the apostle Paul: "For the wrath of God is revealed from heaven against all ungodliness and unrighteousness of men, who suppress the truth in unrighteousness, because what may be known of God is manifest in them, for God has shown it to them."

"Professing to be wise, they became fools" (Rom. 1:18, 19, 22, NKJV).

Alan Watts has stated: "Every Easter Sunday should be celebrated with a solemn and reverent burning of the Holy Scriptures, for the whole meaning of the resurrection and ascension of Christ into heaven (which is within you) is that Godmanhood is to be discovered here and now inwardly, not in the letter of the Bible."[7]

He continues: "In its early ages, the church was in constant expectation of the Parousia, the second coming of the Lord. Obviously, the church has been looking for the Parousia in the wrong direction—in the outward skies not in the realm of heaven which is within. The true Parousia comes at the moment of crisis in consciousness."[8]

With the advocacy of man turning inwardly for understanding and then being told that the "Enlightenment" comes in the form of a void, his rational mind must be discarded and he then becomes the object of manipulation.

Fourth-Dimensional Christianity in Contrast

The Holy Spirit desires to bring the Christian into a familiarity with a new dimension of spirit. He causes us to pray and meditate, not within ourselves, but on the Holy Scriptures. After all, Christianity was not born in a classroom. It was birthed through a dynamically impacting experience with the Holy Spirit at the day of

Pentecost. Therefore, Christianity cannot be a sterile theological exercise. It must be a vitally impacting spiritual relationship with Jesus Christ.

Whereas Zen ignores or condemns the concept of sin, the Holy Spirit delivers us from it through the blood of Jesus Christ. While Zen asks its practitioners to meditate within themselves, the Holy Spirit delivers us from self-centeredness and causes us to be concerned with the needs of others. While Zen says that to attain spiritual perfection is to enter into a voidness of the mind, the Holy Spirit brings us into a personal relationship with Jesus Christ. God, therefore, can be known in an intimate relationship with His Son. While Zen tries to destroy our God-given natural capacity for reason, the Holy Spirit causes our minds to be renewed and rational powers to be sanctified so that we might understand His will for our lives and His glorious creation that He has meant for us to enjoy. While Zen gives man no hope for the future, the Holy Spirit causes us to experience Christ's divine kingdom here on earth with the expectation of experiencing much more for eternity in His divine presence.

While Zen Buddhism causes man to experience self-induced insanity through irrational meditation and abstinence, the Holy Spirit causes men to dream and see visions of God's divine will and become healthier in body, soul and spirit. Zen leads man to despair, but Christ gives us life and that more abundantly. Zen keeps man in ignorance; Christ causes man to know the truth.

Paul prophesied concerning these times: "Now the Spirit expressly says that in latter times some will depart from the faith, giving heed to deceiving spirits and doctrines of demons, speaking lies in hypocrisy, having their own conscience seared with a hot iron, forbidding to marry, and commanding to abstain from foods which God created to be received with thanksgiving by those who believe and know the truth" (1 Tim. 4:1-3, NKJV). Paul clearly saw what it would be like today. He saw Christianity being attacked by false religions. He saw that many of these doctrines would try to make man abstain from normal practices such as marriage and eating.

Yet, we are encouraged by the miracle of Aaron's rod. While Egyptian magicians were able to counterfeit God's miracle, their rods were swallowed up by Aaron's rod. As we approach the end of this age and as we see Satan's work within our society, we are encouraged by knowing that Christ has conquered. Our power is stronger than Satan's power. We are not subject to the devil's trickery, but we are more than conquerers through Jesus Christ our Lord.

3
The Renewing of the Mind

"And do not be conformed to this world, but be transformed by the renewing of your mind, that you may prove what is that good and acceptable and perfect will of God" (Rom. 12:2, NKJV).

One of the greatest mysteries to mankind throughout the centuries has been his most prized and most complicated physical organ, his brain. A man's mind is more than just his physical brain. The mind is the brain at work in consciousness.

How is the mind different from our physical brain? How is the mind affected at conversion by the added influence of the Holy Spirit? Is the mind renewed by the Holy Spirit at once, or is there a process of renewal? How do the brain and the mind function under control of the Holy Spirit as the Christian learns to walk in the fourth dimension? These and other important questions will be addressed in this chapter.

Before we begin our study into the complicated yet

rewarding questions we have stated above, we should analyze the passage which I quoted from the apostle Paul's Letter to the Romans. Paul wrote this letter to the church at Rome before his visit there. This makes the letter very useful in determining Paul's doctrine which was then unaffected by problems in churches which he had founded. After discussing the importance of natural Israel with this mostly Gentile church in chapters 9, 10 and 11, he then begins to tell the Roman Christians how to live.

According to Paul, Christians living in a Roman secular society were not to be conformed to that society. A.T. Robertson comments on this passage: "Do not take this age as your fashion plate."[1] Peer pressure, along with the social pressures brought to bear on the Roman Christian, would want to make him conform to Roman society, which had all the power in the world. However, Paul does not only give an injunction but he also gives the means by which Christians could avoid destructive conformity. He states that Christians are to be transformed by a renewal of the mind. As the mind is renewed, the Christian is able to rest in the will of God, which is good, acceptable and perfect.

The renewal of the mind brings a transformation. The word that Paul uses, which is translated "transformed," is the Greek word *metamorphousthe,* the same word which Matthew used to describe the transfiguration of Jesus Christ. Paul uses the word in his Second Letter to the Corinthians, "But we all, with unveiled face, beholding as in a mirror the glory of the Lord, are being *transformed* into the same image from glory to glory, just as by the Spirit of the Lord" (2 Cor. 3:18, NKJV). In the English language, you have the word *metamorphose* which is used to describe a change of states. This word has its root in the same Greek word we have been discussing.

Therefore, in order for us not to conform we must be transformed. How are we transformed? Our minds must be renewed.

The Mind and the Brain

The concept of the mind is not new to society and I am sure it was not new to Paul. Paul was an educated man and was familiar with Greek poetry and philosophy. This is why he could command the attention of the Athenians at Mars Hill. Democritus of Abdera (460-370 B.C.), a Greek philosopher, wrote extensively on the subject of the mind. He stated that matter was made up of invisible and movable substances. This concept is similar to our present concept of molecules. He saw that the brain was the place where all of the senses and perceptions dwelt. He believed that everything could be explained with more knowledge regarding this human organ. He thereby created a materialistic philosophy. Later, Plato rejected

Democritus' philosophy as amoral and incomplete. If the whole world consisted only of matter composed of atomic particles, then man did not have will and could not be held responsible for his actions.

Paul was very much aware of this controversy and stated simply that the mind could be renewed. In doing so, Paul showed us that the mind was the center of concern. Our actions were to be guided by a transformation of our lives, which would be accomplished by a renewal of the mind. The mind was distinct from our physical brain which housed the senses and consciousness of men.

In order for us to greater understand the differentiation between our mind and brain, we need to know more about both. We are unique in God's creation: He created us in His own image. We are more than what we are physically. We are also more than we can understand about ourselves. Our potential is much greater than our experience. God, viewing man's ability at the Tower of Babel, said that man was capable of doing whatever he was able to envision. If this is so, then even with our great advances in knowledge and technology, we have yet to see man's potential realized.

We have normally understood the verse quoted at the beginning of this chapter as a warning against the Christian remaining or becoming worldly. Yet we can also interpret the verse as a great challenge to the Christian. If this world is to be saved, we must be able to speak the Word of God in the power of the Holy Spirit. The mind of the Christian can not only be renewed for the purpose of not conforming to this world, but it also can be renewed for the sake of realizing our potential as human beings created in the image of God. We can then not be limited to the limits that this world is placing on our knowledge and understanding but we can transcend the limitations. Our ability is only limited by our own limits.

God said of man after the flood that he was capable of doing whatever he envisioned. Could it be that as our minds are renewed, we will have a greater vision? Could it be that the world's greatest problems are awaiting a renewed people who have been able to transcend the self-imposed limits of our present society? Before we address these important questions, let us look at the organ that houses our self, that is, our brain.

The human brain is the most intricate system in the explored universe. Without the protection of the skull, the exposed organ of the brain is the most vulnerable in the human body. It has the consistency of paste and can be severely damaged by only slight pressure. It can also survive severe damage having the ability to transfer crucial functions from damaged to undamaged areas. The combination of structural delicacy and functional ruggedness makes the brain a marvel to the scientific community.

The Brain in Historical Perspective

Men have not always thought that the brain was the center of our mental and emotional activities. The early Greeks thought that thinking took place in the belly. Aristotle thought that the heart was the place where man thought. In Italy, at the University of Bologna in 1637, the first real ideas developed regarding the brain and its functions, using the pooled resources of men and women from all over the world. The information derived from dissecting human cadavers was used by early Renaissance artists such as Leonardo da Vinci.

From early times till today, the brain has been one of the subjects most studied by scientists, doctors and philosophers. Yet, although much is known, many questions are still to be answered.

How Does the Brain Function?

The human central nervous system consists of the brain and the spinal cord. From these two structures branch out a network of fibers, similar to a telephone network, which link the entire body together. The fibers are called nerves. These nerves are one-way paths which either feed information to the central nervous system or carry commands from the system to the whole body. The command-carrying nerves are called the efferent system. These are broken down into two categories: one is voluntary and the other is autonomic. The voluntary nerves control those parts of our body that we can consciously move, such as our muscles. The autonomic nerves control those parts and functions of our body that we do not consciously control, such as the heart, glands and body temperature.

Although the body has many parts and performs many functions, it has only one control center. The fact is that we are only conscious of ourselves as one. We never think of ourselves as primarily a heart, arm, leg, brain or any other distinctive part. This is one reason God has linked our relationship to each other and to himself in terms of a body. The Body of Christ has only one consciousness; we, as each part, can only function as we function under the direction of our head, Jesus Christ. The whole Body is linked together by one system which is the person of the Holy Spirit. He feeds our head the information we send in prayer and then He carries the commands to the several parts of the Body. Some of the commands are voluntary requiring our obedience, but many are automatic, such as His function as the convictor of sin, righteousness, and judgment.

What Is the Brain Like?

Approximately 83 percent of our brain is the neocortex, also known as the cerebral cortex. The brain is divided roughly into two hemispheres, the right and the left. The composition of the brain is made up of cells called neurons. The two halves of the brain are linked through a thick band of axons (the fiber through which neurons communicate) called corpus callosum. The top portion of the neocortex is called the grey matter and the portion underneath is called the white matter.

My purpose is not to give an exact description of the brain's composition. This would be both tedious and cumbersome to many readers of this book. However, a simplified understanding of what the brain is like will help us to understand what I will be describing later.

How Does the Brain Communicate?

The brain communicates through the nervous system by the means of small electrical impulses of about .10 of a volt. The neurons have an ability to not only receive information through these impulses but also to pass along the information throughout the entire system directly to the organs, muscles and senses involved.

The Brain and Blood

Recent studies have provided some new information about the living human brain. It has been observed that blood flow to different parts of the nervous system is delicately and carefully controlled by the vascular system. Neural activity consumes energy just as muscular activity does. An active section of the brain demands more oxygen than does one which is inactive.

Therefore, more blood needs to be rushed to that part of the brain which is engaged in activity.

Scientists in Sweden have observed that, by using a radioactive substance in a person's bloodstream, they can observe the gamma rays coming from the brain. When the patient was at rest, most of the blood was in the frontal cortex. This part of the brain is believed to control our reflections on the past and the ability to creatively plan for the future. This means a great deal to us in understanding the function of our brain. When the same patient was speaking or acting in some way, the blood was more evenly distributed.

Learning how to rest and wait upon the Lord is one of the most important and difficult things that Christians need to learn. Hours spent quietly and prayerfully not only give us perspective and direction but they are now understood to allow the most creative aspect of our brains to work as well.

Waiting on the Lord

Thousands of years before these observations were made, the prophet Isaiah revealed, "Even the youths shall faint and be weary, and the young men shall utterly fall, But those who wait on the LORD shall renew their strength; They shall mount up with wings like eagles, They shall run and not be weary, They shall walk and not faint" (Isa. 40:30, 31, NKJV).

The message of the preceding verses is very clear.

Natural strength as exhibited in youth is not capable of overcoming extreme difficulties. But there is a strength which does not depend on being young. This strength comes from learning to wait upon the Lord.

I have learned that an idea is more valuable than material resources. Obstacles which cannot be overcome by natural resources can be overcome through a creative idea. The problems which humanity has faced in the past have resulted more than anything else from a lack of ideas.

Years ago, in the beautiful city of Helsinki, Finland; the State Church desired to build a church in the downtown area. However, there was no land that could be purchased for this purpose. The only place where there was an open space was in one of the most strategic downtown locations. Yet there was an enormous rock which dominated the area. There was no way to eliminate the rock and the situation seemed hopeless. But two Christian young men waited and got an idea.

"Why not make the church inside the rock?" they thought. Now there exists one of the most beautiful church structures in the entire earth: the Rock Church. Anyone looking from the outside can only see a large boulder, but as you go through the doors you enter into a marvelous church which has also become an important tourist attraction. The solution did not come from trying to remove the obstacle, but digging through it with a creative idea.

Problems which eluded us in the past can be overcome through creative thinking, if we can learn to wait
upon the Lord. Isaiah shows us how waiting works. He
uses a Hebrew word translated "renew" but which can
be better translated "exchange." This means that, by
waiting upon the Lord, we actually exchange our
strength with God's strength. Now this strength does
not only have to be physical. It can be mental as well.
Therefore, as we wait upon the Lord, we can have His
creative strength work upon our minds to give us the
answers to questions we have not been able to resolve.

Since the physical world is a shadow of the spiritual
world, what we know scientifically of the material helps
us in understanding the spiritual. Jesus revealed
spiritual truth by using material examples. The
regeneration which is done by the Holy Spirit at
conversion was referred to in a physical way as being
born again. When describing the spiritual implications
of the kingdom of God, Jesus used the material
mustard seed which is small yet grows into a large
plant. Paul reveals the same principle when teaching
the Corinthian church the importance of the physical
resurrection of Jesus Christ. "Howbeit that was not
first which is spiritual, but that which is natural; and
afterward that which is spiritual." Therefore, our
understanding of the creative thinking in our brain
during times of inactivity only points to the spiritual
implications of waiting upon the Lord.

Scientific Determination versus Randomness

One of the most significant arguments within the scientific community is the argument between the determinists and those that hold to the random theory.

Men like Harvard's Sanford Palay that hold to the determinist point of view have pointed out that the nervous system is not a random net. It is redundant. Its organization is highly specific, not merely in terms of connections between the neurons, but also in terms of the number, style, and location of terminals upon different parts of the same cell and the precise distribution of terminals arising from that cell.

In order for us to understand this position, we must first examine what gives each of us individuality. Each of us has inherited a specific blueprint which is unique to ourselves alone. The blueprint is contained in molecules called DNA (deoxyribonucleic acid). The blueprint is followed not only in our body features, but also in our emotional make-up. We also have other proteins (histocompatibility antigens) which give each of us a distinct selfhood. This genetic selfhood makes up our immune system, which protects us from invasions of foreign bodies. (This is not to be confused with the selfhood we have which is experienced in our consciousness.)

We often have heard of people being given organs from donors to replace organs that have become defective. The greatest difficulty after a successful operation is the natural tendency of the recipient to reject the foreign body because it does not have the same antigen or code. It is as if each of us has been given a code similar to the ones used by banks in order for us to draw money from automatic tellers. If someone tries to make a transaction within your account and they don't have the secret code, the transaction is automatically cancelled.

The wide range of individual codes (if we can continue with the same metaphor) is very large. We see this by looking at identical twins. We know that their genetic blueprints are identical. They may have the same eyes, noses and hands, but their fingerprints will be different. What gives the difference that protects each person individually and causes such a wide variation in the human species?

The determinist believes that there is a reason for the great variation. Although the reason may not be clear at the time, there are physical causes which can be understood in the future. The people that follow the random theory believe that the variety is caused by chance. We will understand this better as we go along.

A question which is of particular interest to us as Christians is how we can all be different and still all be in the image of God. There are several spiritual principles that give us understanding regarding this important question.

The Fourth Dimension

1. *Within unity there is diversity.*

God is one God yet He is three persons: Father, Son and Holy Spirit. His completeness is manifested in the Son who came to this world in the person of Jesus Christ. Yet Jesus depended completely on the Father who gave Him power through the Holy Spirit. Although the complexities of the Trinity cannot be exhaustively understood, we can understand and know Him by Faith.

2. *God has a definite will, yet His ways are beyond our finding out.*

This does not mean that we cannot know the ways of God, but we can never know them exhaustively. Moses knew His ways, but he did not know them all.

3. *God's creation reflects His nature.*

Within all entities there are parts. We are only conscious of ourselves as one. We do not recognize the left and right hemispheres of our brains as distinctive. We only recognize that we are who we are. Yet, experiments have proven that there are two distinct levels of consciousness in the two hemispheres of our brains. Each one has different functions. For example, the left hemisphere has the ability to speak and articulate its thoughts. Yet, everyone has only one identity.

4. *Even matter reflects the principle of unity and diversity.*

As you hold the book you are reading in your hand, you are taking for granted the stability of the paper which has been bound together. Your book is not moving at random in your hands. If you put it down and go to the kitchen to get a cup of coffee, you can be sure that when you come back it will be at the exact location where you placed it, barring an earthquake or an intruder.

Yet you are taking too much for granted! As you look at the paper you are now reading, you are not conscious of the fact that the paper is made up of certain molecules. Each one of those molecules is made up of atoms. And you probably don't realize that the atoms are made up of subatomic particles which are in a constant state of motion. Thanks to quantum mechanics, we now understand much more about the microuniverse which makes up all matter. It is important for us to understand our universe because God created it. The more we know about His creation, the more we appreciate the manifold wisdom of the Creator.

What is quantum mechanics? This new system grew out of observing light waves and X-rays. Scientists saw that they had characteristics of particles under certain circumstances.

In 1925, the French physicist De Broglie stated that

particles, like electrons, had characteristics like waves. Soon, Erwin Schrodinger proposed a new type of mechanics which was able to analyze waves and particles. Niels Bohr proposed that electrons move in an uncertain pattern and their exact location could not be exactly predicted. Therefore, only the probability of where the electrons could be at a certain location could be predicted. For example, we could say that there was a 60 percent chance of it being at a certain place. This poses a serious problem for many scientists in that they try to understand and predict something exactly. But the conclusion now exists that in the world of the subatomic particle, nothing can be predicted exactly.

Some have said that this world exists in a chaotic state. This view holds that nothing can be predicted exactly and that events are guided by chance. However, how can a material universe so exact in so many ways, and so stable, be essentially chaotic? This is a mystery which is still puzzling the scientific world.

Yet when we understand that the universe reflects its Creator, we can have some appreciation for this puzzling phenomenon.

One thing that mathematicians and physicists find difficult to understand is that there are things that are beyond our understanding. Although man has the ability, given by God, to understand, his understanding is only finite and not exhaustive. "The secret things belong unto the LORD our God: but those things which are revealed belong unto us and to our children for ever, that we may do all the words of this law" (Deut. 29:29, KJV).

Another aspect that is of interest to every believer is the power of the Word of our Lord and Savior, Jesus Christ. His Word brought order out of chaos in the beginning. It also holds all things together. This means that the whole material creation is held together not by a mystery, but by His Word. When God said, "Let there be!" that Word not only worked once, but it is still at work. Therefore, randomness may be better understood as unlimited variation. Also, the book that you are presently holding is stable due to a force which is at work making the chaotic subatomic particles into a stable material product. This force is the Word of the Lord and will be explained in the next chapter.

I further understand that to some this answer may seem simplistic in that it is based on faith. Yet faith cannot take the place of knowledge and knowledge cannot take the place of faith.

Scientists have faith in their rational power. We have faith in the Word of God. The two are not necessarily in conflict. We, as Christians, have the distinct ability to understand knowledge within the context of faith. We, therefore, can conclude that there is a difference between two levels of the material world (the perceptible world of matter and the imperceptible world of the subatomic). These two levels are not necessarily in conflict, for the unity of the Creator can overcome the diversity of the smallest level of the creation.

The Mind and Consciousness

We are more than our physical parts. We are more than merely a machine. We are conscious of being a person. We have the ability to see, feel, taste, smell and be concerned. Machines don't concern themselves with worrying about whether they will be kept in good repair or not. They do not have consciousness. Our consciousness is quite complex; it will not serve our purpose to try to go into too detailed an explanation in this section. However, understanding who we are will give us an idea of what and who we are able to become under the Holy Spirit's influence in the fourth dimension.

It is my intention to try to understand with you, my reader, the newest neuroscientific developments as they relate to our sensory perceptions and consciousness, then relate what we are now learning to the Truth about us derived from God's final word, the Scriptures. I must state in this section the fact that I am not a neuroscientist; as a preacher of the gospel, however, I keep abreast of what is happening in the world of science. The reason for this is that I believe that we who proclaim the Word of God have an opportunity and responsibility to unveil reality to the world in a way that the world can understand. I am also a man who enjoys learning more about God and His creation. In doing so, I can help others learn more as well.

Our Senses

Most of what we know consciously comes to us by what we see. Yet our seeing is more than what we actually view with our eyes. We not only see, we also perceive.

For example, suppose you are taking a walk on a lovely day in the fall. You look up at the sky. What do you see? Well, what you see depends to a great deal on your perception, based on what you have learned and experienced in the past. What you are actually seeing is light coming into your eyes. This light is focused on your retina where a neural pattern is created and transmitted to the visual cortex. There the neural code simply reports a message to your brain: "You are seeing white, irregular shapes slowly drifting across a blue background." Yet when you look at the sky you are perceiving much more than just that sensory information.

If you are an artist, you might view the formations of clouds as a beautiful picture worthy to be reproduced on a canvas. If you are a poet, you may be inspired to reflect on a sheet of paper your emotions regarding the scene that you have just witnessed. If you are a weatherman, you may look for signs within the clouds which might foretell a changing weather pattern. Yet no matter what your background may be, you are still looking at the same thing. Perception, therefore, is a vital part of what we call our consciousness. Perception involves not only the gathering of information from our physical senses, but also the integration of the information into logical mental patterns that we can understand and relate to others.

The eye is more than an organ which gives visual information to the brain. In 1975, scientists at Northwestern University tested subjects for what are known as blind spots. Basically, they showed that visual patterns surrounding blind spots are extended through the non-seeing area by the perceiving brain. They also showed that these could also appear in portions of the visual field that are served by a healthy, functioning retina and visual cortex (within the brain). The subjects were able to complete and see visual patterns that were not actually complete. The eye in conjunction with the brain was able to make up the difference. This is also true when we study our sense of hearing. Subjects can listen to a tape and hear a missing word in a sentence. For example, they might hear, "John, please pick up the laundry!" as a complete sentence, while actually the word "up" was left out. Scientists concluded that the brain works with the senses to supply information which is left out. In this way it can present a rational conception of a fact or an event.

This is not to detract from the fact that senses can

receive direct stimuli from the objects being perceived. For example, when one sees water and one is thirsty, the water can produce enough stimuli to cause the person to want to drink it. But the fact still remains that our previous experience and knowledge has a great bearing upon what we know through our senses.

For this reason it is difficult to learn something totally new. We have a tendency to know what we have known because we can relate to it easily from our previous experience. This fact about us has a very important spiritual bearing.

There is an account in Luke 9 which illustrates this very principle. The disciples had just experienced two very remarkable events in the life of Christ. They had seen the Transfiguration of Jesus, heard the voice of approval from the Father and then they saw Christ rebuke unclean spirits from a child. They were very impressed with the Master they had chosen to follow. It was at this time of heightened expectation that Jesus said something very remarkable to them: "Let these sayings sink down into your ears, for the Son of Man is about to be delivered into the hands of men." However, Luke tells us, "But they did not understand this saying, and it was hidden from them so that they did not *perceive* it; and they were afraid to ask Him about that saying" (Luke 9:44, 45, NKJV).

The disciples *heard* what Jesus said, but they did not *perceive* what He said. Their perception of Christ was one of victory, not death. They could not integrate His statement with their experience of seeing Him heal and being glorified. This was why they still did not believe until Christ was resurrected, although He had explained everything to them very clearly.

The Pharisees saw the miracles of Christ, yet they did not perceive them. If Christ had come from better circumstances, if their mind-set had been different regarding the possibility of His being the Messiah; then they would have not only seen, but they would have perceived.

Our attitudes have much to do with our perceptions. If we have no desire to see or to hear, we can often not see and hear, although both of these senses may be otherwise working properly.

Jesus said, "Ye shall know the truth, and the truth shall make you free" (John 8:32, KJV). If we desire to have our minds delivered from the preconceptions that keep us from perceiving reality, then the way has been made. We need to know the truth of the Word of God not only in our minds but also in our experience.

By allowing God to cause us to grow experientially into fourth-dimensional living, we can then have the capability to see and hear what we may have missed, if we did not know His truth.

An example which can make this point clear to us is an experience that a man had in a European museum. This gentleman was knowledgable in the area of art.

He walked through the museum in Florence and was amazed at the beauty of a Michaelangelo sculpture. As he stood away to get a better perspective, another gentleman walked up to the sculpture, looked at it and said to his friend, "Isn't that pretty?" With that, he moved on to see something else. The first man was shocked at the other man's lack of appreciation. When my friend told me the story, I simply asked, "Which one of you saw the work of art?"

The priceless truths of the Word of God have been written for thousands of years. Men from all backgrounds have glanced through the pages or tried to memorize the words, but not many have seen the truths that are in the Scriptures. Why not? Because what we see as well as what we hear is based not only on our ability to read and study the language, but it is based on our mental preconceptions, desires and experience. Jesus said, "For judgment I am come into this world, that they which see not might see; and that they which see might be made blind" (John 9:39).

Therefore, our minds can be renewed by allowing the Holy Spirit to change our preconceptions, attitudes and desires. He also guides us in our lives towards experiences which will cause us to have a basis from which we will be able to see. This is the process of maturity in the Christian. We cannot add any more to this subject than the explanation that is given in Hebrews: "For though by this time you ought to be teachers, you need someone to teach you again the first principles of the oracles of God; and you have come to need milk and not solid food.

"For everyone who partakes only of milk is unskilled in the word of righteousness, for he is a babe. But solid food belongs to those who are of full age, that is, those who by reason of use have their senses exercised to discern both good and evil" (Heb. 5:12-14, NKJV).

Mental Simulation

Before an artist begins to paint, he first forms a mental image which he draws upon a sketchpad. If we follow the idea carefully, we notice certain important facts. The idea begins in the mind of the artist and is then projected upon the pad. However, the same mind that thought of the idea and was able to sketch the idea on the pad is also able to examine it and make additions or deletions. The artist may like or dislike the idea, but he has the capacity to judge and improve it because he has sketched it out first.

In the same way, Bach needed a musical instrument to play the composition before he could judge it, all those who create in any medium need to create a simulation of thought in an external way in order to judge that thought.

Language has a similar function. When we talk to ourselves or think out loud, we may not be crazy, but we may actually be clarifying our thinking, which cannot be analyzed while it still remains silent in our mind. Psychologists now believe that children develop language skills not so much by speaking to others, but by talking to themselves.

The mind has the ability to hold and analyze thought only for a relatively short period of time. We can examine thoughts and images in our minds. But these do not last; therefore, protracted contemplation is not possible. The mind's ability to do this is called mental simulation.

Where and how are these images stored and analyzed? The answer to this question is still not completely known. However, it is now believed that this is done in the part of the brain which controls our sight. It seems that the mind has an internal mechanism in which images are produced as thoughts. In the next chapter we shall see that a proper exercise of language can be to use words to produce the same image within the person's mind that you may have in yours. This principle has rich spiritual meaning for us in this book.

As we discussed in the previous chapter, one of the principles of fourth-dimensional life is learning to speak the language of the Holy Spirit, which is visions and dreams.

How does the Holy Spirit use visions and dreams in communicating with us? We saw in the previous chapter examples of Abraham, Joseph and others using this principle. But here our desire is to try to understand how this principle actually works.

If our thinking is a series of pictures which take place in the area of our minds that is involved in our speech, and if the Holy Spirit works within the Christian to communicate to him the will of God, then He communicates to his mind in the area where he thinks. If we have an internal sketchpad which we use as a reference point to write, play an instrument or speak, then this same sketchpad can be used by the Holy Spirit to give us God's direction.

The problem exists of distinguishing the voice of the Holy Spirit from other voices. For this reason we need to rely solely on the Word of God, which gives us the will of God. However, the sketchpad is also available to be used by the believer in developing the mindset which will guide his future actions.

I have often said that to accomplish something we have to see it first. This is because our bodies will fall into line with that which is going on in our minds. We can actually participate in the fulfillment of the will of God communicated to us by the Holy Spirit by taking the paint brush of the will of God, dipping it into the ink of faith and beginning to draw pictures of His will on the canvas or sketchpad of our imagination. Our imagination is then that sketchpad that plays such an important role in our lives and is such an integral part of our conscious actions.

Athletes claim that they have to first picture the accomplishment of a certain play before they actually can perform it properly. This is mental simulation at work. Therefore, the same principles which neuroscientists are now studying have been in the Word of God for thousands of years. Remember the previous chapter when we spoke of Abraham looking at the stars in response to the command of God? He pictured his children as a countless number. He used mental simulation to draw a mental picture in his imagination which eventually was able to control his ability to produce a child with his wife Sarah.

Volition

Nothing is more precious to man in his conscious state than his ability to exercise his will. The freedom to exercise his will has been something that man has been willing to die for.

Nineteenth-century materialists believed that since man was only a highly complex machine, his free will was only a mental delusion. All that was happening when he thought that he was acting was that the machine was responding to external stimuli along with his own chemical and physiological state. Fortunately, that view is today in decline.

Yet what is free will? What is really happening when we decide to do something? These questions are at once very complicated and very important.

The Fourth Dimension

When a man does something or desires to do something, he has to be motivated. That motivation may not be rational but it is certainly actual. If something or someone is restricting his ability to act freely, he then focuses on that restriction and has to decide either to fight it, try to remove it or just submit to the restriction and possibly wait until he is able to act freely.

There is also another aspect of volition which is part of our state of consciousness: we have a feeling of being free. Man has known little that lifts his spirit more than the ability to walk outside and feel free. In the 13th century Dante said, "The greatest gift that God in His bounty made in creation, and the most conformable to His goodness, and that which He prizes the most, was the freedom of the will, with which the creatures with intelligence, they all and they alone were and are endowed."

I recently read of an interesting study which related to this subject. This study was conducted in 1976 by a group of scientists in Germany. They placed electrodes on the brains of a group of volunteers and traced the impulses coming from the brain as the subjects were asked to voluntarily move their fingers. Amazingly, there were impulses in the brain as much as one second before the subjects voluntarily and freely moved their fingers. Was something triggered in their minds that they were not conscious of before they exercised their freedom to move their fingers? Apparently. If, when we act freely, we are actually doing something without being caused to do it by an external force, then, perhaps we may not be as free as we have been led by our feelings to believe.

The subject of freedom is still a mystery to many who have not trusted the Word of God. Even in the believing community we have had controversy concerning our freedom. Since the beginning of the Church people have wondered whether we accepted Christ because we wanted to or we simply did what we were predetermined, by God, to do. Obviously, this question will not be resolved in this book; however, we can understand something about our freedom from Paul's Letter to the Philippians: ". . . work out your own salvation with fear and trembling; for it is God who works in you both to will and to do for His good pleasure" (Phil. 2:12, 13).

Paul commands the church at Philippi to work out their own salvation with a deep sense of responsibility. We cannot consciously blame someone or something else for our actions. If we act, we are then responsible for our actions. When, however, you examine your actions further, you see that many times things seem to happen beyond your understanding. We seem to act freely, but our actions fall into a perfect pattern we could never know naturally.

God is at work in us both in our actions and, more

importantly, in our motivations. The Holy Spirit, when He enters into our lives, begins to motivate us to do the will of God. Yet, even before we are Christians, the Holy Spirit is arranging the circumstances under which we will hear the gospel and believe. Remember that the Holy Spirit was sent to the world to convict of sin, righteousness and judgment. He was working on us before we ever allowed Him to enter into us. This does not mean that we are not responsible if we disobey. God holds us responsible for our actions. But we have been given all of the stimuli necessary for us to do the will of God.

Other experiments in this area have shown that we are not always conscious of what is going on inside our minds and what our senses are telling us. Therefore we must rely on the Word of God which never changes.

Finally, we seem to have two levels of actions. One level of acting freely is the conscious action. That is, we act knowing exactly why we are acting. The other is the act in which we do not know exactly why we act, only we feel like performing that particular act. We may call one rational, and the other emotional. However, both, if we are able to perform them without outside stimuli or restriction, are free acts of will. Yet, we have been made from two parents from which we have inherited not only looks but also personality and predispositions. We are also products of our environment, which influences our behavior. But for the Christian, the most important thing is to recognize the importance of filling our minds with the Word of God, so that our natural predisposition for action will be in accordance with the truth of the Scriptures.

"Thy Word have I hid in mine heart, that I might not sin against Thee" (Ps. 119:11, KJV). If it is true that there are motivational forces at work in our minds which trigger actions which we feel are totally free even for impulsive acts of our will, then it is extremely important to let that motivational force be the Holy Spirit. The Holy Spirit will then trigger responses in our minds that have been predetermined by the Word of God. In this way we may be able to lead lives that are both pleasing and productive.

The renewed mind is a mind that will be able to discern the will of God which is pleasing, acceptable and perfect. We will not feel like accidents waiting to happen, but our lives will be ordered and directed to the goals that we know are the will of God. Our energies and resources will not be sapped by irrelevant activity, but our resources will be trained upon the perfect will of God in our lives.

A renewed mind will change our lifestyle. We will no longer live meaninglessly, but the purpose which we are geared to accomplish will cause us to be happy, healthy and productive Christians. Our minds can then guide our words and our words will have a great effect on our actions. This is why you need to read the next chapter.

4
The Creative Ability of Your Words

Did you know that your words were creative? They are either creative in a positive or negative way. They can produce life or death. Words have a power much greater than most of us can understand today. Psychologists, medical doctors and philosophers are just starting to understand what the Bible has been telling us for thousands of years: "For we all stumble in many things. If anyone does not stumble in word, he is a perfect man, able also to bridle the whole body" (James 3:2, NKJV). The truth given to us in this verse is very important; it enables us to see the impact our words have upon our whole being. James gives us three basic facts about the power of our words:

1. *Words can be uncontrollable.*

How many times have you said something only to later regret having said it? So often our emotions have more control over our words than our logic. We have a tendency to react to someone who has gotten us upset and we say something back that later we feel terrible about. Therefore, James tells us that we stumble over our words.

Our words also can be motivated by our insecurity. Many ministers are guilty of exaggeration. This is due to the fact that preachers receive their approval not from monetary remuneration, but from crowd acceptance. Therefore, by embellishing a story, fact or event, they stand to gain even greater approval from the crowd.

Our words can be greatly influenced by our associations. If we associate with negative people, we will find our words becoming more negative than normal.

Our words can be controlled by our imagination. Whatever we dwell upon, we will speak. If we daydream about things that are of the flesh, then out of our mouths we will find words coming that will refer to fleshly things and which will be beyond our control.

2. *What indicates a perfect, or, more accurately stated, a mature man?*

A mature person is one who is able to control his words. This, of course, does not justify those people who find it easy to say nothing. However, James tells us that if someone is so disciplined that he is able to control his speech, he is then mature. The Greek word *teleos* (perfect) means mature or fully tested. But the word translated man is not the more common *anthropos,* but the word *aner.* Kittel states that in classical Greek, this particular use of the word signifies man as opposed to woman.[1] He also states that in the New Testament the word signifies husband.[2] Robertson agrees with Kittel and translates the verse as "perfect husband."[3]

Those who have been married understand perfectly what James is implying in this verse. If your words are not going to be cautious, they will be so with your spouse. However, the general principle is also true for all people.

3. *The way to control your body and to avoid its misuse is to control your words.*

James likens the proper control of the tongue to the control of a horse. He uses the word "bridle." In a well-trained horse, a bridle can serve to either start, stop or change a horse's direction when it is used to exert a small amount of pressure in the horse's mouth. The part of the bridle that is doing the work is not easily visible, but it can dramatically affect the horse's behavior. So too our words. They seem so insignificantly uttered, but they have such great consequences upon us physically, emotionally and spiritually.

James uses the metaphor of a ship's rudder in the fourth verse. Winds, currents and sails do not ultimately determine the direction that a sailing vessel will go.

The direction will be determined by a small rudder which is not seen but which nonetheless exercises great influence.

The point that James is making by using these two powerful examples is that whatever is in control of your words will control you. If you do not bring your words under your control, your life will be lived as a stumbling horse, directionless and accomplishing very little. Yet a mature spiritual man will make sure that his words are positive and creative. He will not allow himself to be controlled by circumstances, but will control his circumstances because he knows where he is going. He will use his words wisely.

What Are Words?

Although we accept the importance of our words, we have to have an understanding of what words are. After all, as Christians, we are people who are verbally oriented. We believe in the Word (Jesus Christ) according to John 1:1-3. We also accept that the basic force that keeps everything in the physical world together is a word from the Word, "who being the brightness of His glory and the express image of His person, and [upholds] all things by the word of His power . . ." (Heb. 1:3, NKJV). Our faith is based on trusting in a God who is revealed to our hearts by the Holy Spirit. We accept the truth of a book (the Bible) which is full of words. Yet these words are more than ink on paper; they are the Word of God. Christ challenged us to go into all the world and preach the good news. Therefore, we are people who believe in propagating our faith through the use of words. No other group of people on earth should be more interested in understanding what words are and how they can be used more effectively.

Within the past hundred years many people have been challenged to understand exactly what words are. One of the fathers of modern linguistics, F. de Saussure (a French-Swiss) stated, "The function of language builds on the complex interplay between objective (physical) and subjective (mental) elements. Sounds, such as physical activities, are employed as symbols of meaning which is what ultimately establishes language as a mental rather than a physical phenomenon."[4] Saussure continues, "Everything in language is basically psychological."[5]

What Saussure is basically saying is that words are more than what we say. They begin in the mind as thoughts. This is why people who are mutes can use words in sign language. Although they cannot speak, they can communicate ideas by using physical actions which signify understandable words.

Psychologists have been interested in this subject ever since Wilhelm Wendt (1832-1920) coined the term "psycholinguistics." Believing that by understanding the psychological aspects of words, they might be able to understand the way man's mind functions, he tried to use methods by which he could understand the relationship between ideas and phonomes (words as physical sounds).

Interest in words is not new. Plato gave his ideas concerning the nature of words in his dialogues. St. Augustine stated that every word had a meaning and that sentences were merely a combination of these meanings. However, the study of the psychological, physical and emotional impact of words is basically new to scientists. Much of the philosophy of the West has concentrated on defining what words mean. Ludwig Wittgenstein, however, became skeptical of this practice and stated that objects could never be defined too specifically because of the nature of change within language. The inability to give exact definitions of words caused him to want to understand what words were in essence. "What really comes before our mind when we understand a word?" he asked. "Isn't it something like a picture? Can't it [the word] be a picture?"[6] What Wittgenstein believed is that our understanding comes in the area of our imagination. When we picture something in our mind we understand it. That, in essence, is the definition of that thing. The word sound which is uttered may not be able to fully communicate that picture, but the purpose of communication is to convey the picture to someone else as completely as possible.

Therefore, we understand that words begin in the mind. We visualize something and we associate a phonome with it. The word exists in our mind before it is ever spoken. When we speak, there is a dynamic added to the concept we visualize, for the sound of the word may also add meaning to the word spoken.

In Chinese the same word can have different meanings, depending on the way the word is spoken. The tone that is used and the inflection of the voice lend an added dimension to what is said.

Children understand this concept very well. Having three children, I have learned much from being a father. One of my three boys was still getting dressed as we were on our way to a church dinner. The rest of us were dressed and still waiting for him. I went into his room and yelled, "Hurry up!" He, being quite young, began to cry. I could have used exactly the same words with a different tone and his reaction would have been much different. He knew what I was trying to communicate to him. My words stated a command; I wanted him to hurry. But the tone of my voice stated, "Hurry up! You have made me upset and you are going to be spanked!"

Words are described by John William Miller as symbols to grasp understanding. Words therefore reproduce the picture that the speaker is conveying in the mind of the hearer. He states that art is also a symbol in that it too tries to communicate ideas or pictures in the artist's mind by the use of a symbol (a work of art).

The Word in the New Testament Greek Language

The word translated "speaking" (*lego*) and the word translated "thinking" (*logismos*) both, according to Kittel, have their roots in the Greek word *logos*.[7] Therefore, what we have previously discussed concerning the psychological aspects of words were already in the minds of the Greeks; the idea of the relationship between thinking, speaking and writing is not new.

The word *logos* in the Greek language has a rich meaning and history. It originally had several nuances which were used by John to describe our Lord.

Some of the developmental meanings of the word *logos* are:

a. the collecting of information
b. the counting or reckoning of something
c. mathematical calculations used in accounting
d. the evaluation of facts
e. From the previous meanings the word developed into: the assessment of things in general and their correlation. (This is where we get the word "catalogue" in English.)

    f. During the time of Homer the word had the meaning of the reasonable explanation of something.

    g. After the ancient Greek poets, *logos* takes on the meaning of speaking, replacing the previous word, *epos*.

The reason the word changed was because the people changed. As philosophers took a more important role in the lives of the Greek people, they in turn affected the language. Since reason and logic were important to the Greek people, the word signifying "speaking" was then developed from a word whose previous meanings included "the gathering of information" and "the presenting of facts." This had a different nuance than other words such as *epos* and *rama,* which described speech. These two were concerned more with the phonetic implications rather than the reasoning of the philosopher. "The causing of something to be seen for what it is, and the possibility of being oriented thereby is the meaning of logos," Aristotle stated.

Later on, the word *logos* is used in relation to the mythological god, Hermes. Hermes, in mythology, was the mediator between all the other gods. He was the revealer of truth. Therefore, during the Hellenistic period, *logos* took on a significantly religious connotation. The secular Greek use of *logos* was quite different from the New Testament use of the word, specifically as it refers to Jesus Christ in John's Gospel.

Words Carry the Weight of the Speaker

H. Meyer, a New Testament scholar, believes that the Greek work *logos* had an implied meaning based on the importance of the person speaking. The more important the person, the weightier his words. The principle which Meyer states is true today. If the president of a country makes a speech, his words will carry more weight in that country than if an ordinary citizen states the same thing.

Jesus Christ, being the Son of God and the Redeemer of the world, spoke with such weight that His words produced life. If what was spoken by Jesus was repeated by anyone else, in another name, then his words would not be as powerful. The implication of this principle is that words not only convey meaning, but they also convey the character and personality of the speaker.

Since our words come from within our heart, they divulge the very intent of our thinking. This is why it is not what goes into a man's mouth that defiles him, but what comes out of his mouth. The person speaking a word, or words in a sentence, has to understand the importance of what he is saying, especially if he is a prominent person. People who are highly regarded are going to be heard.

The Creative Ability of Your Words

In Korea, I am well known by almost everyone in the whole nation. When I speak, people listen and take what I say very seriously. Since I have never thought of myself as being better or more important than anyone else, I have had a difficult time adjusting to the fact that people are closely listening to my words, especially those words which I speak casually. I have learned that I cannot jest openly. I have to watch what I say. If I were to say something casually in jest, people would take me seriously and spread it all over the country. So I have learned to watch my words for I know that other people are listening to me intently.

The speaker's importance is an additional factor in his word because of the dimension of the speaker's authority. The masses in Israel listened to Christ by the hillside and by the lake and they also listened to the priests in the temple. The comparison that they made was that Christ's words were different, for He spoke as one having authority.

When someone says something, the authority of the individual will determine the degree to which what he says will be obeyed and remembered. The Roman centurion told Jesus that he understood military principles. He was not worthy that Christ should come under his roof, knowing that a Jew could not defile himself by going into the home of a Gentile. But he said that he was under authority and therefore he exercised authority. Taking for granted that the spiritual kingdom of Christ functioned under the same principles as Rome, he then told Christ to simply speak the word and his servant would be healed (Matt. 8:8). Jesus marvelled at the Roman's understanding of spiritual reality, for He had offered to go to his home and had promised the healing. What greater honor could be bestowed on anyone. Yet the centurion knew that only a word (*logos*) was needed for the miracle to take place. He recognized the authority with which Jesus spoke. This does not mean that Jesus spoke in an overly loud voice. At times, those with the least authority speak loudly because of their insecurity. But when someone has authority, that authority is transmitted by the way in which he speaks. Those who hear one who is speaking in such a manner will comprehend the weight of what is spoken, although additional language may not be added.

The Word of God

In Acts 6, we learn that the Apostles realized that they were not to be involved in the daily administration of the needs of the saints, but their job was to study and teach the Word (*logos*) of God. This truth seems to be lost to much of the ministry today. So many preachers spend more time in their offices doing administrative work than in the Word of God. The fact is that the Word of God has many dimensions which cannot be comprehended by only a single reading. The Bible (God's Word) is not just a piece of literature. It cannot be read once, understood and then taught to others. The Word of God is many-sided and must be studied over and over again.

The Spirit of Truth has come to lead and guide us into all truth. How does He guide us? He, the Holy Spirit, knows the mind of God. He is, therefore, able to explain what was in God's mind when God spoke, both in the Old Testament (through the prophets) and in the New Testament (through the Apostles). If we understand that words do not fully and exhaustively explain the mental picture, then it is helpful to have someone who knows the inner working of the mind of the person who spoke. Therefore, it is imperative that we have the Holy Spirit leading and guiding us through the study of the Scriptures.

If the word which is spoken carries the weight of the speaker, then the *logos* of God has a spiritual as well as an intellectual dynamic which makes that word special. If God has told us (in James) that we should be careful in our use of words, then it is certain that God has been careful in the use of every word which has been written in the Scriptures. If words are to convey a mental picture, then we should learn how to visualize the Word of God and try to understand what He sees. We most assuredly need the Holy Spirit in order to do this. Since the Holy Spirit was the one who caused the prophets to speak ("For prophecy never came by the will of man, but holy men of God spoke as they were moved [borne gently] by the Holy Spirit"—2 Pet. 1:21, NKJV), He then is able to interpret best what they said.

Jesus said that the Holy Spirit came upon the prophets as they spoke in the Old Testament. These prophecies were spoken as the Holy Spirit moved the prophets to speak. And these very words are called the Word of God or Scripture (Mark 12:10; 15:28; Luke 4:21; John 7:38; Acts 8:32, etc.). Yet the Word of God found in the Old Testament and the Word of God spoken by our Lord are not the only words called Scripture; the New Testament also is the Word of God: "Therefore, beloved, looking forward to these things, be diligent to be found by Him in peace, without spot and blameless; and account that the longsuffering of our Lord is salvation—as also our beloved brother Paul, according to the wisdom given to him, has written to you, as also in all his epistles, speaking in them of these things, in which are some things hard to understand, which those who are untaught and unstable twist to their own destruction, as they do also the *rest of the Scriptures*" (2 Pet. 3:14-16, NKJV). Therefore, the same Holy Spirit that came upon the prophets and moved them to speak also moved the writers in the New Testament, but from a different location. Jesus promised that the Holy Spirit would be inside the believer.

As the Holy Spirit has invaded human beings who believe in the Lord Jesus Christ, He is not occasionally coming upon us, but He lives the life of Christ in us. This Holy Spirit can cause us to see what was not seen, even by the prophets who heard God speak and faithfully spoke for God, as recounted in the Old Testament. Therefore it was imperative that Christ depart so He could send another Comforter, the Holy Spirit. This is why it is so important for us to depend upon the Holy Spirit as we endeavor in a deeper way to understand God's Word. Paul said, "But we speak the wisdom of God in a mystery, the hidden wisdom which God ordained before the ages for our glory, which none of the rulers of this age knew; for had they known, they would not have crucified the Lord of glory. But as it is written: 'Eye has not seen, nor ear heard, nor have entered into the heart of man the things which God has prepared for those how love Him.' But God has revealed them to us through His Spirit. For the Spirit searches all things, yes, the deep things of God" (1 Cor. 2:7-10, NKJV).

Although the Old Testament is full of the Word of God coming to the prophets, there are only two instances in the New Testament that the Holy Spirit came in the same way (to Simeon and John the Baptist). We are told that the Holy Spirit directed Simeon to the temple at the same time that Jesus was to be presented before the Lord God. (See Luke 2:25-30.) As he saw the Christ child, he was moved by the Holy Spirit and began to prophesy. John the Baptist was also moved by the Holy Spirit in the wilderness to begin his prophetic ministry. The term used in the Greek is *rema Theon*. The Word of God came upon him. These are the last two times in the New Testament that God spoke to man in this way. Kittel says, "The phrases *logos tou Theou, logos tou kuriou* and *rema kuriou* (Greek for 'the Word of God' and 'the Word of the Lord') are very common in the New Testament, but, except in the case of these introductory figures (Simeon and John), they are never used of special divine directions. It is not that these do not occur in the New Testament. On the contrary, the apostolic age is full of them. But they are described in many other different ways."[8] The conclusion can therefore be drawn that since the coming of the Lord, who is the Word of God, the Word of God would never come again in the same way. Jesus never received the Word of God because He was the Word of God. Everything that had ever been said by God through the prophets in the past represented only a partial revelation of truth; with the coming of Christ, however, the whole of truth was revealed in a Person. The only times God spoke from heaven (at the Mount of Transfiguration and at Christ's water baptism), the audience was not Christ, but those who were watching God bear witness of Him.

It is not that God would not speak prophetically through His servants in the New Testament, but that there would be a difference in their prophetic ministry.

Therefore, Jesus spoke the Word of God as the Word of God. The prophetic realm is a limited one: "For we know in part and we prophesy in part. But when that which is perfect has come, then that which is in part will be done away" (1 Cor. 13:9, 10, NKJV).

How can we speak the Word of God in a complete way? Peter gives us the answer: "For we did not follow cunningly devised fables when we made known to you the power and coming of our Lord Jesus Christ, but were eyewitnesses of His majesty. For He received from God the Father honor and glory when such a voice came to Him from the Excellent Glory: 'This is My beloved Son, in whom I am well pleased.' And we heard this voice which came from heaven when we were with Him on the holy mountain. We also have the prophetic word made more sure, which you do well to heed as a light that shines in a dark place, until the day dawns and the morning star rises in your hearts; knowing this first, that no prophecy of Scripture is of any private interpretation" (2 Peter 1:16-20, NKJV).

Words which are written have a more permanent nature than those that are spoken. My people have learned that misunderstandings can arise when they communicate by phone only, but when they write a letter, which can be answered by a letter, then there is a permanent record of the communicated information. Our faith does not depend on an oral tradition, as many other religions have. God spoke in the Old Testament and what God wanted us to know was written down. God speaks to us today through the Scriptures, both Old and New Testaments. Peter states that this record is more reliable than actually hearing the voice of God personally. He compares the voice he heard at the Mount of Transfiguration with the record in Scripture and says that the record is a more sure Word of prophecy. This does not mean that man cannot prophesy today. But it does mean that when we speak the Word of God from Scripture, that Word is complete and not partial.

Words Have Power

Solomon said: "Death and life are in the power of the tongue" (Prov. 18:21).

In volume 1 of *The Fourth Dimension,* I wrote about a neuro-surgeon who told me about a new discovery in his field. By now, that principle is a well-established fact. The speech center in the brain has direct influence over the entire nervous system. Solomon, thousands of years before the discovery which science has made in recent years, stated the very same fact. In surgery, the will of the patient to pull through his operation will have as much to do with the success of the operation as any other external factor. The will of the patient will not only give the body of the patient the ability to stay alive during the operation, but will actually aid in the healing process. That will is affected by what the patient confesses. If he confesses death, then death will begin to work in his system. If he confesses life, the body begins to release the natural forces of healing to make that confession true.

This truth is especially important for older people. One of the most debilitating factors in contemporary society is forced retirement at what is frequently the still productive age of sixty-five. This is just when a person begins to learn about life, just when the cumulative experiences of a lifetime can be most useful. To be forced to go out to pasture at such a time can be disastrous. The mind then starts to think of itself as old and will begin to confess, "I'm retired now. I am too old to do anything productive." The body will respond to those words and begin to age more rapidly. This does not mean that all retired people are unproductive or are forced to retire because they are no longer of use. But it does seem like that to many retired people. They miss years of being useful to God and their society because they feel that they are "too old" and ineffectual. Age is more than chronology; it is a state of mind. That mind is influenced by the words which are spoken.

Poverty is a curse from Satan. God desires that all His people prosper and be healthy as their soul prospers (3 John 1:2). Yet much of the world has not really seen poverty as I have seen it. Especially in the Third World, people live their lives in despair, struggling to survive for one more day. I am from the

Third World. I know first-hand what it is not to have anything to eat. My country was ravaged by the Japanese for many years; then we suffered through two wars. Korea is just now rising up economically. Why? One of the reasons we are succeeding and prospering materially is because we are changing our self-image as a nation. While under Japanese colonial rule we found it difficult to have a good self-image and national dignity. But, against great odds, we were able to maintain our language, culture and national identity.

When I started my church, we had just seen the end to the Korean Conflict. Our people struggled just to eat. I then saw that God wanted to bless us materially as a testimony to His grace and power. This does not mean that economically underprivileged Christians are second-class citizens. But it does mean that we have to believe that the blessing of God is part of His redemptive provision.

I then started to see the importance of teaching my people the power and substance of their confession. If we confessed we were poor and created a poor self-image by our confession, we would always be poor and in need of material help and handouts from the West. But by trusting in God and working very hard, our people were able to lift themselves from the depths of poverty into a place where they could bless the work of God in our country and throughout the world.

The Creative Ability of Your Words

Last year, I spoke at our Church Growth Conference in Sri Lanka. Previously called Ceylon, that nation is one of the poorest countries in the world. The bulk of my ministry was spent teaching them how to change their self-image. They had to realize that God is their source, not America and Europe. The main way a group of people can change their self-image is by carefully using words which are positive and which produce dignity within both the speaker and the hearer. Reports are still coming back about the results of that conference which brought together about five hundred Christian leaders from all Christian denominations.

In Mark's Gospel, we have a very beautiful and interesting narrative which reveals the potential power of our words as Christians. After Jesus had returned from His triumphal entry into Jerusalem He went directly to the temple. He saw what was going on but said nothing. He left Jerusalem to spend the night at the home of friends in Bethany. The next morning, He was hurrying and approached a fig tree that had large lovely leaves. Looking under the leaves for the fruit He saw nothing. The tree looked productive, but had produced no fruit. Jesus then cursed the tree and went on back into Jerusalem to cleanse the temple.

Since no action taken by Christ in the Scripture is without meaning, the tree, of course, symbolized Israel. Upon the disciples' return to the area where the tree was, however, Peter looked at the tree and said,

"Rabbi, look! The fig tree which you cursed has withered away." Rather than dealing with the symbolic significance of the tree withering, that they could know the principle that that which cannot bear fruit shouldn't make the appearance of health; Jesus dealt with Peter's surprise at His ability to produce a miracle. This should be surprising to us because Peter had seen Christ perform many more spectacular miracles in the past. However, Jesus used this occasion to reveal the potential power of our words as Christians.

"For assuredly, I say to you, whoever says to this mountain, 'Be removed and be cast into the sea,' and does not doubt in his heart, but believes that those things he *says* will come to pass, he will have whatever he *says*" (Mark 11:23, NKJV). Merely *thinking* our words does not produce the miracle; the miracle is produced by *saying* what you believe. Christ promised that we could only have what we confessed. The story of the mountain being physically removed is only to add emphasis to the ability of the spoken word. If we as Christians only knew what power we can release when we speak in faith, we would be using our words more effectively.

Our words are important. Malachi tells us that God keeps a book of remembrance. Daniel was told by the angel Gabriel that he had come for his words. Paul tells us that God's redemptive word of salvation climaxes when we confess Jesus Christ as our Savior. The heart believes unto righteousness. You can be righteous in your heart, but words are necessary for you to be saved. Only thinking in faith will not release the power of God; we must learn to speak in faith. Our words are creative either for good or for evil. God has given all the grace necessary for us to learn to use our words creatively for the purpose of seeing His kingdom established in this earth.

How to Develop a Creative Word

As we look at the Genesis account of the creation, we can understand how God used His words creatively. Before God said, "Let there be . . . ," He had a clear goal and objective. As we understand by looking carefully at the story of the creation in Genesis, everything was created from the earth's perspective. But why should God create from this perspective since the universe is so vast, with many billions of stars larger than our own sun?

The reason for choosing the earth was that this planet was the place where man would dwell. If it were not for this goal, that is, creating a perfect place for man, the earth would be like any other planet, incapable of supporting human life.

Paul shows man's central purpose not only in the earth but also in the universe. He says in Romans 8 that the whole of creation was placed in a decaying process by the sin of Adam, but when man finally comes to the place of total victory and redemption, the creation, which has been waiting in hope, will be set free. The physical law, called by science "entropy," will be reversed even as we see our bodies overcome the process at the end of the age.

In the Letter to the Colossians, Paul reinforces the fact that Christ was the means by which everything, either visible or invisible, was created. Yet Paul immediately links Christ to His physical body on earth, the Church. In Ephesians, Paul states that we were in Christ before the worlds were founded. He then closes the first chapter by stating that we are His fullness which fills all in all. In the Greek text, this passage has even more significance than is obvious in the translation we are using. A more literal translation can be, "fills all that is capable of being filled." The obvious inference is that the Church, filled with Christ's glory, then fulfills His ultimate purpose of having the whole of creation filled with His glory. Our ultimate influence, therefore, is not just limited to this earth, but is intended for the whole of God's creation.

Seeing that we were in God's mind before the world was created, we can then understand the purpose of God choosing to create this planet capable of sustaining human life.

In learning to use our creative words, we must take our lesson from God. So often we speak in faith, but we don't have a clear objective. We don't know where we are going because we live from day to day. You may ask, didn't the Lord tell us to live like this? This is true, but He was dealing with those who worry. I am not speaking about worry. I am speaking about having a clear objective and goal for the future which you have received from the Holy Spirit.

When God said, "Let there be . . .," He already knew the end of the matter. He saw clearly all of us, not as we are, but as we will be in Christ. He then had a clear objective: He would create a planet for the purpose of having a perfect place for man to inhabit.

Yet before God ever spoke, the Holy Spirit was working in the area of His desire. The Holy Spirit was creating the circumstances which would bring about what God would say. This fact must be very clear if we are ever going to learn how to use our creative language. We must learn to walk in the Holy Spirit and have Him direct us in what God desires. Once we get our instructions from the Holy Spirit, we can speak to our chaotic situations and circumstances with authority and we will see things begin to happen.

I was once invited to a church banquet and at this lovely dinner I used this very principle. One of our elders had a son who had an incurable paralysis which was getting progressively worse. As I was sitting at the table, the Lord spoke to me: "Get up and go to your elder and tell him that tonight his son will be completely healed!" I then began to be fearful in my heart. My wife turned to me and said, "What is wrong with you?" When I told her, she put her hand on my arm and said, "Don't you dare do that! You know that he has been prayed for many times. What if nothing happens? You will be ruined in this church." I agreed with her wisdom but got up anyway. (I have learned that it is better to obey the Holy Spirit at the risk of failure than never to try to see the glory of God manifested.) As I approached the elder, I smiled as he asked me, "What can I do for you, pastor?" I then breathed deeply and plunged into my statement: "The Holy Spirit just told me to tell you that tonight your son will be healed." Once I had obeyed, I felt total and complete relief. He then told his wife and the two of them began to cry out thanksgiving to God. Before long, everyone knew what I had shared with the elder and they too were praising God.

Once I sat down, my heart sank. What would be the consequences if nothing happened? But it was too late.

That night, the couple went directly to the boy's room and told him what I had said. He tried to get out of bed, but could not. They prayed and he tried again, but still his condition remained the same. Finally, the father said to God, "Lord, you told our pastor tonight that our son would be healed. He is a man of God and we believe him. We know that you would not ask him to say that unless you meant to perform a miracle." With that, the father took his son's arm, pulled him out of the bed and said, "In the name of Jesus, rise up and walk!"

As the child stood on his legs, his limbs were strengthened. He stood up and began to run all over the room. The news of that miracle spread all over their community; because of that testimony many families were saved.

In our society we are faced with chaos all around us, just as the earth was chaotic (without form and void) before God spoke. As we learn to walk in obedience to the Holy Spirit, we will learn to use the creative ability of our words to bring order out of chaos.

Our words can make the difference if we learn to use them effectively. We can either spend our Christian lives without proper control over our words, or we will see their importance, power and creativity and use them for the purpose that God originally intended. Let your words be positive and productive. Meditate upon positive and creative things. Fill your mind with the Word of God and you will be able to see the Word of God coming forth from your lips naturally. "Let the words of my mouth, and the meditation of my heart, be acceptable in Thy sight, O LORD, my strength, and my redeemer" (Ps. 19:14, KJV).

5

Love: The Motivational Force

What motivates you to do what you do? This is an important question which Christians need to explore. Psychologists have been interested for many years about what basically motivates human behavior. We understand that our actions are motivated by differing forces. Some are motivated by power, others by the need to have money, and still others are driven by their creative instincts. This is particularly true of artists who are willing to sacrifice materially in order to create within the areas of their interest. But, what is it that motivates us as Christians to break through the usual into the unusual, the natural plane of life into the supernatural, the three-dimensional lifestyle into the fourth dimension? What will cause us to put into practice those truths which I have previously shared in this book? This is what we are going to explore in this chapter.

Before we explain how we are motivated, we need to

understand what motivation is. "Motivation is a term used to cover explanations of why a person behaves as he does. It is not synonymous with 'causation' because it is generally restricted to only one class of events determining behavior. For example, it is commonly contrasted with ability, another determinant of behavior: a person may be able to play a game of tennis, but he may not want to; i.e., he is not motivated to play. Or on the other hand, he may want to and not be able to. Both ability and desire jointly determine what he actually does. Motivation is ordinarily indicated by such words as want, wish, desire, need and strive."[1]

In classical Greek thinking, the soul of man was divided into three parts: reason, and then two other parts which controlled his motivation. These two parts were his will and desire. Sigmund Freud taught his pupils that man had three parts. The three parts of man all worked together to form his personality and govern his actions. These were the id, the ego and the superego. Freud believed that the superego motivated man to perform his most noble acts, the id was the opposite force working against the superego and the ego was that balancing force which mediated between the other forces so that the person would act in a rational manner. C.G. Jung did not agree with Freud because he felt that Freud's concepts of man did not explain in enough detail the motivational forces of an artist's creativity.

Love: The Motivational Force

Today, both sociologists and psychologists are more interested in practical aspects of motivation. Studies have been made to try to understand what causes some people to perform better than others of equal ability. If industry can understand what motivates people most effectively, an individual's productive capacity can be increased dramatically. Recent books have noted that the reason for low productivity within industrial nations can be attributed to the change of incentives within their economies. In the past, when most people lived on farms, a man was motivated to plant crops because he was able to reap his own harvest. The fall harvest made the work in the spring and summer worthwhile. Then there was a mass migration into urban areas in which men were no longer rewarded by harvests, but instead by paychecks and fringe benefits. With increased industrial specialization a worker would often not see the finished product, which he had only a small part in creating. The pride which a worker could take in his work was replaced by money. With increased leisure time available in the form of longer vacations, a person who previously had an investment of ego within his work, came to look at his job only as a means of earning money to do other things. Increased salaries and benefits did not produce greater productivity because of the loss of motivation. Now, industry is trying to understand what really motivates workers to produce better products. The answer is not money.

The Fourth Dimension

Educators are also vitally interested in trying to understand motivation. It is now understood that an important relationship exists between motivation and cognition. Students will learn and retain to a greater degree those things that they feel will be of practical use to them. Therefore, new techniques are being introduced into early school years which will seek to understand a child's motivational pattern and then provide specialized training in that area along with the liberal arts necessary to complete his education.

Although we as Christians are affected by the same motivational forces which affect the world, we have a greater and more powerful force at our disposal. We are not just citizens of this world. Our citizenship transcends the kingdoms of this world and brings us under the rulership of the kingdom of God. The Apostle Paul said, "He has delivered us from the power of darkness and translated us into the kingdom of the Son of His Love" (Col. 1:13, NKJV). We are not limited to this world's resources, but we are joint heirs with the Christ of eternal resources. Through the eternal motivational force of the kingdom of God, we are capable of doing more and enduring more than those who are depending on the limited resources of this world. This unlimited force which can and should motivate all of our behavior is the Love of God.

The Love of God: His Motivational Force

Probably the most familiar verse in the New Testament is, "For God so loved the world that He gave His only begotten Son, that whoever believes in Him should not perish but have everlasting life" (John 3:16, NKJV).

W. Frank Scott in his "Homiletical Commentary" states concerning this verse: "John is veritably the apostle of love. He alone of all the apostolic band seems to have been chosen to understand somewhat the depths of this divine love, so that he might tell it to men. The spirit of inspiration chooses fitting instruments; and we must assume that by nature and grace St. John was best fitted to make known the gospel of this eternal spring. Its presence had been implied before, when the revelation of Christ was spoken of; but now it is clearly made known."

The eternal spring that Scott refers to is the motivational force that caused God to sacrifice His only begotten Son, Jesus Christ. Why would the Father give His all not only for Israel, the Church, but the whole world? The answer is His Love. In order to understand the motivating force which caused God to sacrifice His Son, we must look carefully at His love. What is the Love of God? It is His essence. God does not love as an act, He loves out of His own essence. He does not try to love; His love is natural. "He who does not love does not know God, for God is love" (1 John 4:8, NKJV).

151

His actions are not motivated by sentiment but by His nature: God is Love.

During the time of Christ, the Old Testament was the subject of much controversy. Daily there were arguments concerning the finer points of the law. The Pharisees had one point of view, the Sadducees another. At one point, a lawyer, who was also a Pharisee asked Christ a question which he did not think had an acceptable answer. "Teacher, which is the great commandment in the law?" the lawyer asked, knowing that Christ could be stuck if He merely tried to answer the question. After all, if all the commandments were from God, who could put a value judgment upon them? By choosing one, he would reduce the others to a lesser position. But Christ had no difficulty with the answer and did not hesitate: "You shall love the Lord your God with all your mind; this is the first and great commandment. And the second is like it: You shall love your neighbor as yourself. On these two commandments hang all the Law and the Prophets." Instead of placing a value judgment on the commandments which God had given to Moses, Christ summarized all of them by giving the essence of what God desires His people to do: love Him and love others. Jesus also summarized and condensed the entire Old Testament into these two commands, which John reveals later are really one. John asks, "How can you love God who you can't see and hate your brother who you can see?

Therefore, it is impossible to love God and hate your brother."

Since the great commandment was given by our Lord, men have been trying to divide the one into two. In some liberal churches, the great emphasis is on loving people. In some conservative churches, the command is to love God. History records horrors against groups of people that have been committed by people, who say that they love God, against groups of people who believed differently. Yet some of the people that do most for other people often fail in their personal devotion to Jesus Christ. Jesus Christ taught that to truly obey God, one must do both. I have discovered in my twenty-seven years of ministry that when I am most loving to God, I am also most loving to His people.

Seemingly, some liberal groups have left the preaching of the Scriptures and have become little more than social welfare agencies. People come to these churches to be fed spiritually and all they receive is self-justifying platitudes. It seems that their only reason for meeting and collecting offerings is to do social work. This is not the Love of God. Human love is motivated by a sense of duty and sympathy; the love of God is motivated by the Holy Spirit. But some conservative Christian churches are preaching the gospel of salvation from sin, but are not too concerned about the people's physical needs. They may spend hours praying and worshiping God, yet are oblivious to those that are needy. The love of God brings balance! It causes us to serve God and love Him faithfully, but does not ignore those who are in need. The New Testament church is revealed to us through the Book of Acts. Luke shows how the early church loved God faithfully, and were also willing to sacrifice their material possessions to meet the needs of those in their group who were suffering materially.

Studying church history reveals that every great revival has been followed by a change in the social order of the people affected by the revival. For example, the revival which brought into being the Methodist church saved Great Britian from the revolutionary upheaval suffered in France. With the genuine spiritual renewal of the church came a greater awareness of the suffering of the English masses. New organizations designed to help the needy were founded. An example of such an organization is the Salvation Army, founded by William Booth in 1865. This organization was founded as a result of a new social awareness created by a spiritual awakening which previously swept Great Britain. Organizations such as the Red Cross were started around the same time. Once the love of God flows into us, it must naturally flow out to others!

What Is Love?

Everyone thinks they know what the word love means, but it is widely misunderstood. In our culture, the word is thought of as an act rather than an attitude. We have perverted the word from its original biblical concept and returned to the Greek concepts of love which are foreign to Scripture. For us to understand the love of God, we must look at the difference between the Greek and the scriptural concept of the word.

1. *Love's intensity.*

"You shall love the Lord your God with all your heart, with all your soul, and with all your might" (Deut. 5:5). Modern man says, "I love you because you are now doing good things for me." But this type of love involves little permanence and only temporary commitment. God revealed the intensity of love when He commanded Israel to love Him. There are several implications which can be derived from the verse which I just quoted:

a. The Love of God can be willed.

God will never require His people to do anything which they are incapable of doing. If God said, "You shall love," that means that we are capable of loving by choosing to love. Western culture's concept of love has been affected by the Romantic Era. During this time people thought that loving was something that was purely emotional and had nothing to do with an act of the will. As we shall see later, the Love of God is not emotional, although it can be felt emotionally. Therefore, we can choose to love as an act of obedience to God.

b. Love is complete.

God commanded Israel to love Him with all, not some, of their heart. Israel could not save a bit of love for some other god; God required everything.

c. Love is an act of the heart, mind (soul), and will (might).

Although love begins in the heart as a response, it also includes the mind. We are given many instances in Scripture where God reasons with the people of Israel and gives them logical reasons why they should love Him. Circumstances change, misunderstandings arise, yet love is also kept alive by an act of our might. Sometimes loving someone is inconvenient, but when we choose to love, we love regardless of the circumstances. Using might in love is not common within human relationships that are founded on emotional responses. But the love of God is more than emotional; it is eternal.

Our natural inclination is to love someone when they produce for us. I often say that we have a natural tendency to write good things others do for us on tablets of water, but bad things are written on tablets of stone. In baseball the saying is true that the crowd forgets the last home run after you strike out. Yet God has commanded His people to a higher level of love. Jesus took love a step further when He gave us a new commandment. He said that it was nothing special to love our friends. After all, this is a common response. He commanded us to love our enemies. This kind of love is not common because it is not natural. God has set the example by loving the world. The world is at enmity with God, Paul reveals. Therefore, the natural world is actively fighting God. It is the world that God loved so much that he gave His Son. God did not wait until the world started loving Him before He sacrificed His Son. He took the initiative.

Love and Covenant

The basis for love in the Scriptures is the covenant relationship between God and His people. A covenant is a legal agreement between two parties. Each party promises to perform a certain duty in exchange for something from the other party. In Deuteronomy, Moses retells the story of the covenant God made with Israel at Sinai. Basically, God promised to give Israel the land which had been promised to their fathers if Israel would keep His commandments. Along with the land was to come protection from their enemies, material blessings and prosperity, and physical growth and standing as a nation. Since the great commandment was to love God unconditionally, eternally, exclusively and intensively, they made an agreement that both could and would keep. God then became their God, and in turn, Israel became His people. Based on this binding agreement, we understand the essence of God's love. Choice is not involved. Feelings and emotions are peripheral aspects of the relationship. God loved us because He chose to. Our response is not based on anything else but an act of obedience. This does not mean that emotional responses to God cannot be involved, but it means that with or without them, our actions are to be loving.

God has made a covenant to love us. This covenant is natural since He is love. Although mercy, pity, kindness, charity and forgiveness are all aspects of His love for us, His primary determination comes out of fulfilling His covenant to love us. This concept of love will become much clearer to us as we understand the Greek word *agape,* which is the word chosen to distinguish the love of God from all other forms of human love commonly understood when the New Testament was written.

Love and Fidelity

Not only is the love of God experienced and known in a juridical way, as in the covenants, but it is also known from a basis of commitment and fidelity. The obvious example of this aspect of the love of God is the fidelity which is commonly expected in marriage.

Being loyal and faithful is something which is still expected in a marriage. Although our worldly age has experimented with what is called "open marriages," these experiments have proven to be total and complete failures. Man is created in the image of God. Marriage was instituted by God himself. Even the non-believer has to look to the Scriptures when he desires to understand the normative behavior expected in a marriage. A man leaves his father and mother and cleaves unto his wife. This principle is as true today as it was when Moses first wrote it. But, the faithfulness which is expected in marriage universally is only a shadow of the relationship of love which God has chosen to have with His people.

"And it shall be, in the day," says the Lord, "that you will call Me 'My Husband,' and no longer call me 'My Master' " (Hos. 2:16, NKJV). Paul gives us the fulfillment of that promise when he states, "For this reason a man shall leave his father and mother and be joined to his wife, and the two shall become one flesh. This is a great mystery, but I speak concerning Christ and the church" (Eph. 5:31, 32, NKJV). The example for the husband is Christ. He loves, protects, supports and gives himself to His people. The example for the wife is the church. She is to love, obey, respect and give herself only to Him. The love which the two share can be maintained by the faithfulness which they have with each other. The relationship is more than emotional. It is legal. They have rights to one another and those rights are protected by a covenant made within the marriage vows. When the heat of their emotional love wanes, they can still maintain their relationship because it is based on a commitment that is eternal. Moses said that writs of divorce were given to Israel because of their unbelief. However, in the love relationship between Christ and the church there is no divorce. Their relationship is eternal.

The Three Greek Words Translated Love

In pre-biblical Greek, there were three words which were used to convey the meaning of love. These three words are *eros, phileo,* and *agape.*

1. Eros: *This word simply means strong passion.*

What many are calling the sexual revolution is not new. The Greeks lived for passion. This can be seen in the writings of Plato in which he spent a good deal of time discussing love as passion. Many of the Greek poems and stories dealt with the intoxication of *eros.* Even the Greek gods fell in love with each other and passionately desired humans. These gods were not served out of devotion but out of fear. They were not perfect examples of purity and chastity, but were subject to the same frailties which were so common to humans.

Eros was so unlike the love which God expects from His people that the word is never used in the New Testament. This does not mean that passion has no place within the marriage relationship, but the concept of passion as an ungovernable intoxication with another person is strictly foreign to the Bible. It is no accident that the Scriptures ignore the most common word for love in classical Greek writings. No! The writers of the New Testament were only too aware of the Greek concepts of love. They were repugnant and repulsive to any believing Jew. This is why there was such an aversion to preaching the gospel to the Greeks. This is why it took a special call to a special apostle to first bring the message of Christ into Macedonia.

Paul had to write to the Corinthians that they should not allow the popular attitudes of the world to affect them in any way. Those who had accepted Christ and His teaching had to purify their lives and avoid the behavior characteristic of contemporary Greek society which practiced things that Paul states are not even to be mentioned among God's people.

2. Phileo: *a genuine friendship or kindness based on a relationship of fondness.*

Another common word, which is also used in the New Testament is the word, *phileo.* It is often translated as brotherly love. The word was used when Plato wished to describe the attitude that one should have towards his community. The word described what was considered the most noble of feelings. It did not carry the intoxications and excesses of *eros,* but described the attitude that would bring the most admiration from others. In classical Greece, men were challenged to open themselves up to others so that they could develop their personality; this was called *phileo.*

During the exchange between Christ and Peter after the resurrection, both *phileo* and *agape* are used. When Christ challenges Peter by pointing to the other disciples and asking, "Do you *agape* me more than these others?" Peter responded, "You know that I *phileo* you."

3. Agape: *a particular word with an unusual background in classical Greek which has special significance as the love of God.*

The etymology of *agape* is not very certain in classical Greek. The word never carried the passion or emotion of *eros,* and it also never carried the nobility of *phileo.* Originally used to express a preference for something or someone, the word developed in an unusual way. *Agape* was used to express a determination of the will to prefer something. With little exception, the word was not used a great deal by Greek poets, who were more interested in exploring subjects of more popular interest. When Plotinus used *agape,* it was used in reference to an act of kindness more than to a strong feeling of emotion.

Therefore, it is not surprising that the Holy Spirit would take an obscure Greek word and inspire the New Testament writers to use it so often and importantly in the New Testament. In this way, descriptions of the love of God would not carry by implication Greek concepts or practices. God could take a word and refine its meaning so that it would give understanding to His essence and His requirements.

Love and the Ministry of Jesus

The life and ministry of Jesus Christ not only fulfilled the will of God by becoming the means and channel by which lost humanity could approach the Father, but He also revealed the Father. By looking at the life of Christ, we could understand what the Father was like. In the Old Testament, we see God the Father dispensing commands and requiring obedience. His justice had to be satisfied through sacrifice. Although God has not changed, the Old Testament only gives us a partial understanding of His nature. Christ came to give us a complete understanding of the Father. He reveals the Father's love and mercy.

It was unfortunate that those who knew His word most understood His nature least. This is why Jesus said, "You see me, you see the Father." Christ did not come to destroy the Law, but to bring it to fulfillment. In doing so, He satisfied the righteousness of God. Now man could have free access to His presence, for the way to His presence had been made clear through Christ.

Christ revolutionized the concept of love. By asking us to *agape* God, He was telling us to serve Him with actions of obedience based on our relationship and not just based on our temporary emotional feelings.

Jesus broke with Jewish tradition when He told the righteous young and rich man that he should sell everything and follow Him as a disciple. Jesus told him, "You cannot serve God and Mammon." The rich young ruler was faithful in following the Law. He paid his tithes and in the eyes of those who followed Christ was a perfect candidate for discipleship. Yet Christ knew that loving God demanded sacrifice. Not that having possessions was wrong. But it was a matter of priorities. To love God was to serve Him, and you cannot serve two masters. Material possessions would be acceptable as long as they were held loosely.

Jesus revealed in Matthew 6, the demands of *agape* love. The rich young man would have an opportunity which would bring him historical importance. If he had been willing to rid himself of his great possessions, he might have been greatly used by God, like Peter or John. But he could not understand the demands of *agape*. He became the only person to be given an opportunity to become a disciple by choice; all the rest were called without an opportunity being given to choose whether to follow or not. The important matter of this story is not the ability of a Christian to have wealth. The main point of this story is the exclusive service which love demands when we decide to become His disciple.

It is God's desire for us to prosper and have a sufficient amount of all good things. But *agape* love demands total and complete service.

Love versus Pride or Vainglory

Jesus referred to the Pharisees in many places in the Gospels. He was most concerned about the religious piety which they practiced which was without the content of godly actions (see His admonition to them in Luke 11:43). They were generous in their giving in that they regularly paid tithes, but because they displayed their giving for all to see, they had no eternal reward.

James makes the point very clearly, "Whoever therefore wants to be a friend of the world makes himself an enemy of God. Or do you think that the Scripture says in vain, 'The Spirit who dwells in us yearns jealously'? But He gives more grace. Therefore He says: 'God resists the proud, but gives grace to the humble' " (James 4:4-6, NKJV).

The Apostle Paul makes the love of God clear in his letter to the Corinthian church. In the first letter, Paul is dealing with a major problem within the church. This was an overemphasis on spiritual gifts and an underemphasis on spiritual fruit. In chapter twelve, Paul reveals the ministry of the Holy Spirit through the Body of Christ. Since they were all members of one body, they should not concern themselves with questions of preeminence. After all, the foot is not jealous of the hand, etc. He ends the chapter preparing the church for "a more excellent way" (1 Cor. 12:31). It is important that we see clearly that at no time does Paul say that what is going to follow is a more excellent thing, just a more excellent way.

So many have misunderstood chapter thirteen (the love chapter). I have heard and read chapter thirteen being regarded as more important than chapters twelve or fourteen. This is not so. Love is not a better gift than faith, healing or tongues. After all, love is not a gift. It is the fruit of the Holy Spirit. What Paul is going to teach the Corinthian church is a better motivation for exercising the gifts of the Holy Spirit. This new motivation is love. When you love, you don't concern yourself with who is in the limelight. It makes no difference if you don't get to preach or prophesy. You are more concerned with the Holy Spirit ministering to the whole Body of Christ than whether you are seen, heard, or not noticed at all.

Paul makes very clear in this chapter that our motivation for exercising every gift including faith has to be out of love. Then he goes on to define love not as a dictionary would define it, but by describing how love behaves. Paul states fourteen facts about love in this chapter. There are five positive facts about love and nine facts which show how love does not behave.

The positive facts are that love:

1. suffers long
2. is kind
3. rejoices in truth
4. bears all
5. believes all

On the other hand, love:

1. does not envy
2. does not parade itself
3. is not puffed up
4. is not rude
5. is not self-serving
6. is not easily provoked
7. thinks no evil
8. doesn't rejoice in iniquity
9. never fails

If a Christian has these fourteen qualities in his ministry and in his lifestyle, he is then emulating the God that he loves, because God is love. That person is not only manifesting the nature, personality and essence of God, but he is also a person whom others will enjoy as well. How often have we met people who sounded spiritual, were gifted and educated in the Scriptures, but were not enjoyable, pleasant people? Although they may sacrifice all and be very dedicated, Paul states that it doesn't profit them anything, since they do not have love.

The motivation which the Christian should then have is the love of God which is shed abroad in our hearts by the Holy Spirit. This motivation will allow a person to break through spiritually as well as in their normal lives. Without the love of God, all the spiritual endeavors will profit very little.

Why should we be desirous of entering into a fourth-dimensional reality and learning how to speak the language of the Holy Spirit? First, we love God and desire to know Him. Paul expressed this motivation in his Epistle to the Philippians: "But indeed I also count all things loss for the excellence of the knowledge of Christ Jesus my Lord, for whom I have suffered the loss of all things, and count them as rubbish, that I may gain Christ and be found in Him, not having my own righteousness, which is from the law, but that which is through faith in Christ, the righteousness which is from God by faith; that I may know Him and the power of His resurrection and the fellowship of his sufferings, being conformed to His death, if, by any means, I may attain to the resurrection from the dead." Paul then continues: "Brethren, I do not count myself to have apprehended; but one thing I do, forgetting those things which are behind and reaching forward to those things which are ahead, I press toward the goal for the prize of the upward call of God in Christ Jesus" (Phil. 3:8-11, 13, 14, NKJV).

Not only did Paul express his personal motivation, but he reveals what he desires for those that are following Christ because of his ministry: "For this reason I bow my knees to the Father of our Lord Jesus Christ, from whom the whole family in heaven and earth is named, that He would grant you, according to the riches of His glory, to be strengthened with might through His Spirit in the inner man, that Christ may dwell in your hearts through faith; that you, being *rooted and grounded in love,* may be able to comprehend with all the saints what is the width and length and depth and height—to know the love of Christ which passes knowledge; that you may be *filled* with *all the fullness of God"*(Eph. 3:14-19, NKJV, emphasis mine).

Second, we are motivated spiritually because of our love for God's people. "We know that we have passed from death to life, because we love the brethren" (1 John 3:14, NKJV). Peter also emphasizes the importance of being motivated to new spiritual heights because of our love for our brothers and sisters in Christ when he states, "Since you have purified your souls in obeying the truth through the Spirit in sincere love of the brethren, love one another fervently with a pure heart" (1 Pet. 1:22, NKJV).

The Fourth Dimension

In the past two decades we have seen clear trends in the way society has been motivated. In the sixties, there was a massive rebellion against established principles of behavior and governmental authority. Men thought that they could change everything and that change would be beneficial. In the seventies, there was a turning to the self, as men tried to concentrate on what was best for them as individuals. This period of time can be called the "what's good for me" generation. The great causes and concerns of the sixties were given up if they proved too costly to the individual aspirations which were thought to be important. World-wide, bookstores were filled with "how-to" books in improving and building self-confidence. The church was also subject to many of the forces of social change which took place in the world. Yet God's Word has not changed. What has been true in the past is still true! God demands love, not only for himself, but also for His people.

What motivates me personally to sacrifice my life for the sake of the gospel is the love of God. This love is directed towards God by the Holy Spirit and then directed outwardly towards His people by the same Holy Spirit.

I am now incubating in my fourth-dimensional visions and dreams half a million members in my church by the end of 1984. Why do I incubate these people in the realm of my imagination? Because I know without a doubt that the best thing that can happen to my community, my nation and the world is for the church of Jesus Christ to be strong and powerful. We are the salt of the earth and without the church, the world would have no hope at all.

Overcoming by Love

As a young man, I was full of feelings of inferiority. I did not feel I was able to do anything significant in this world. I came from a poor area and was not highly educated. I had tuberculosis and therefore my body was not strong. I had little to hope for. Yet I was captivated by the love of God.

I discovered that one can take refuge in self-doubt and self-pity. Pride will keep a person with inferiority complexes from breaking out of his personal problems and beginning to dream great things. Once I fell in love with the Lord Jesus Christ, and His Holy Spirit started directing the love of God towards His people, I could no longer hide within myself. I had to step out in faith and believe God for greater things.

Now I am incubating half a million members in my church by 1984. If you had asked me ten years ago if I thought this was possible, I would have laughed. But I am highly motivated to believe God for what He has promised me. I am also believing for a greater outreach of our missions program all over the world. Not that I believe that God hasn't called other ministries into the world harvest at the end of this age, but I know that God has challenged us to work as if we were the only ones. In order for us to accomplish all of the goals that God has set before me, I cannot afford to feel inadequate or inferior.

It would be very easy for me to settle down now on the accomplishments of the past twenty-five years. I can rest because of the cell system. All of the thousands of members are well taken care of because the cell leaders give personal attention to each saint. Yet I am busier now than ever. I not only preach up to seven times on Sunday, but I also travel throughout the world in Church Growth Conferences. Why don't I rest at home and take it easy? The answer is the love of God.

I have learned to see the fields of harvest. I have talked to the Lord of the Harvest, the Holy Spirit. He has given me a love for each ear of wheat, each church that needs to be encouraged and strengthened. I cannot rest in complacency. I have overcome because of the love of God.

In this day, we see many of God's servants discouraged because they are not seeing what they were believing for. As I travel, I meet many of these people who have lost their hope. I recently received a letter from an American minister that said, "Pastor Cho, I was discouraged and had lost hope. My church was not growing although I tried everything. Then I saw your television program and started to hope again. Now I have changed, my ministry has changed and my church is growing." This pastor had lost his hope and had become discouraged. He did not know the importance of cultivating his hope in love.

Paul shares the key to hope with the Romans: "Now hope does not disappoint, because the love of God has been poured out in our hearts by the Holy Spirit who was given to us" (Rom. 5:5, NKJV).

The basis of discouragement for most ministers is the opposition and criticism they receive even though they are trying to do the best job they can. Once they react to their circumstances without the love which is shed in their hearts by the Holy Spirit on a continual basis, they lose their hope. Their ministry then becomes mechanical and the people who are hungry for truth and reality are not fed.

By understanding the love of God and being motivated by it, you and I can overcome discouragement and hopelessness. God's love causes us to act and not react. God's love causes us not to be satisfied with the approval ratings given by people, but the approval of the Holy Spirit. God's love causes us to love our critics. God's love causes us to see beyond the present trial and look at the goal of our faith. As we learn to walk in love, we rekindle the hope without which it is impossible to build anything.

When a farmer plants his fields, he plants in hope. When a builder lays a foundation, he does it in hope.

When an artist prepares a canvas, he does so in hope. Therefore, when you do anything, either secular or religious, you must do so in hope.

The farmer visualizes the harvest even though all he can see is an empty field of dirt. Most of his work is done before he can see anything which will reward his labor. Yet when the first blades begin to break through the soil, he waits patiently until the fruit of his field is ready for harvest. There are many things that can happen to prevent a successful harvest. There may be a drought or a flood. Yet the farmer cannot worry about these possible problems; he must work as if all will work out well.

Therefore, hopelessness and discouragement can be overcome by the love of God. Paul was the subject of much criticism and had to defend his ministry on numerous occasions. However, when writing to the Corinthians he said, "For we do not commend ourselves again to you, but give you opportunity to glory on our behalf, that you may have something to answer those who glory in appearance and not in heart. For we are beside ourselves, it is for God; or if we are of sound mind, it is for you. *For the love of Christ constrains us,*" (2 Cor. 5:12-14, emphasis mine). Paul had learned that the love of God was the great constrainer against the natural reactions that he would have against his accusers plus the ambivalence which he felt at the time.

Since *agape* love is sacrificial love, and since it needs

no reciprocation, the love of God constrains our natural reactions which cause so many of our conflicts. To love is to be set free. To love is to act as an agent of the Holy Spirit and not react to circumstances and people. To love is to enter a place of existence which causes us to be unshackled from the fears and frustrations which dominate this world.

Overcoming Anxiety Through Love

It is a fact of modern society that most people suffer from increased anxiety-caused pressure and stress. Every day, millions get in cars, buses or trains and head downtown to work. Traffic, noise and pressure of getting to work on time cause people to begin their day full of stress. Jobs are more complex and demanding. With our present economic changes, the fear of losing your job and joining the ranks of the unemployed looms as a large problem to many today.

Those of us who travel a great deal know the pressures of airline schedules. Plane connections can be missed if your plane arrives late and the connecting flight departs on time. I often see people at airports rushing, their adrenalin flowing, facial muscles tight, and obviously suffering from anxiety.

The American Academy of Family Physicians recently released the findings of a study which showed that two-thirds of office visits to family doctors are prompted by stress-related symptoms. It is believed that up to $75 billion a year is lost by American businesses because of lowered productivity, absenteeism and medical costs due directly to stress-related symptoms. Anxiety is now accepted by the medical community as a major contributor to coronary heart disease, cancer, lung ailments, accidental injuries and even suicide. Recent drug reports indicate that the three leading drugs sold in the U.S. are an ulcer medication, a drug for hypertension and a tranquilizer.

The change in society's value systems has been a major contributor to the epidemic we are facing in anxiety-related ailments. Psychiatrists have discovered that the unclear sexual roles caused by today's changing moral values are the main cause of problems between couples. Doctors have also discovered that the stress that anxiety produces and the adrenalin which the body secretes as a natural defense mechanism can become addictive. For example, children who enjoy racing their automobiles in a dangerous manner, students who have to wait until the last day before preparing for an exam, businessmen who purposely function on very tight schedules can be addicted to their own adrenalin.

Thoman Holmes of the University of Washington discovered that people who were anxious were more susceptible to disease than those who were not. He also noted that those who were about to face a situation which they feared or were anxious about, were more likely to come down with a cold or some other illness. The body produces antibodies which combat germs that enter into its system, but when the body faces stress, the natural combatants are retarded and the body is less resistant to attacks by germs and viruses.

Anxiety and stress is not just a Western problem. In today's changing world, the problems that we face in our modern society are also increasingly becoming universal. Finding the answers to overcoming the anxiety and stress epidemic is important for all people in every part of the world. Increasingly, our present communications system has brought the world closer together than ever before. The world is facing a time when more people feel alone in the midst of a population explosion. People feel that they have less control over their lives. Computers and the numbers that we all have to memorize have depersonalized our societies.

A University of California study showed last year that a large number of people suffer from anxiety because they feel they have no control over the circumstances of their lives. Dr. Robert Karasek, professor at Columbia University in New York City has found that people who have little control over their jobs and face tight schedules suffer a greater risk of heart attack than those who have decision-making responsibilities.

How can we overcome anxiety and stress in a world

that is plagued by both? The answer is found in the Scriptures.

Although we live in this world system, we are not of it. We have been given the power to overcome. God commanded His people Israel not to be partakers of the fears that the nations which surrounded them were plagued by (Isa. 8:12, 13). Israel was told by the prophet that natural alliances and the thinking which was common in Syria, the nation with which Israel was negotiating a treaty, was not going to help them if the enemy attacked them. Their safety was in sanctifying the God of Israel. By doing so, they would not have the worry and fear which then surrounded them.

University of Michigan's Louis Ferman found out that a man who had been laid off in 1962 and again in the early seventies and now again from Chrysler was able to overcome the fear and anxiety that has gripped many who are unemployed in the auto industry in Detroit. His secret was that he went to church every Sunday and was strengthened by his faith. What Dr. Ferman has discovered is not new to the Christian who knows the Word of God.

Jesus prophesied in Luke that men's hearts would fail because of fear. What Jesus prophesied in the first century is now medical knowledge. Fear is one of the chief causes of heart attacks. If we can overcome fear, we can overcome anxiety, stress and worry. The fear that our families will have to go hungry if we lose our jobs, the fear that we will be dishonored by not being able to provide for our own, has caused many in this time of depression and recession to turn to alcohol, pills and tranquilizers.

The Apostle John revealed the ground where fear cannot stand upon: the perfect love of God. "There is no fear in love; but perfect love casteth out fear: because fear hath torment. He that feareth is not made perfect in love" (1 John 4:18, NKJV). Therefore we have the way we can overcome fear.

As the lack of control over our lives causes us to fear that we are hopelessly alone and produces anxiety, so the love of God gives us the confidence that God is in control over all of our circumstances. The love of God gives us purpose and meaning beyond that purpose and meaning that is universally known. We know that because God loved us individually and died for our personal and individual sins, we are therefore significant and important. The love of God gives us the confidence that all things are working together for our good because we love God and are called according to His purpose. We are not accidents waiting to happen. We have a calling and a destiny which is significant.

Since so much of the stress and anxiety that the world suffers comes from interpersonal relationships. The love of God is the answer. By not only knowing the love of God toward us, but then sharing this love with others, we do not have to live lives that are confrontational. We can treat everyone as we would like to be treated. As we do that, we find that people will respond. So often people are just as afraid of us as we are of them. They are waiting for someone to break the ice. Warmth and friendship can come forth out of impersonal situations. If you are in a crowded elevator, you will find people just looking up and staring at the numbers. People are afraid to smile and act friendly. However, the love of God does not need reciprocity. You can be a committee of one to smile and say something friendly. More times than not, others will smile back and the nonpersonal situation can change for everyone.

In our urban centers, people often live in apartments next to neighbors for years before they get to know each other. As so much of stress and anxiety is related to a sense of alienation, this can be overcome by the love of God which can begin through you.

Love also causes us to walk in forgiveness. By not allowing resentment and anger to dwell in our hearts, we can build ourselves emotionally. Therefore, when the natural stresses of life affect us, we have the emotional resources to combat them successfully. If Christ told us to forgive seventy times seven each day, how often will He forgive us? We cannot allow ourselves to be kept back by thinking about the past and our previous mistakes. The past is forgiven by the mercy and grace of our Lord Jesus Christ and the future is in His hands, so the only time that we can concern ourselves with is the present. I have discovered that people who are guilty because of sin which they do not feel forgiven from, will have a difficult time forgiving others. Therefore, the first step to learning to forgive is knowing that we are forgiven.

As we are certain and secure in the forgiveness which Christ has given to us, we can then live out the rest of our lives practicing forgiveness. As we forgive, the tensions that can arise from others wronging us automatically disappear and we avoid the fear, anxiety and stress that comes from broken relationships. The love of God will cause us to realize with Paul that we have been called into a ministry of reconciliation. Again, Christ is our example. He became sin for us who knew no sin, that we might be made the very righteousness of God. The message of the cross is the message of reconciliation. Our lives should be lived reconciling men to God. When you realize that your job is only part of your responsibility and that you have the ministry of reconciler, then there is no room for fear and anxiety.

The love of God will not only cause us to be motivated to do the will of God, living as fourth-dimensional Christians, but it will also be the means by which we can live healthy and successful lives.

Notes

Chapter Two

1. Altizer, *Oriental Mysticism and Biblical Eschatology,* pp. 11, 107.

2. Arnold Toynbee, *Civilization on Trial,* p. 262.

3. Albert Schweitzer, *The Philosophy of Civilization.*

4. Philip Schaff, *History of the Christian Church,* 2:109.

5. C.G. Jung, *Modern Man in Search of a Soul.*

6. D.T. Suzuki, *Selected Writings* (on Zen), p. 15.

7. Alan Watts, *Beyond Theology: The Art of Godmanship,* p. 115.

8. Ibid., p. 164.

Chapter Four

1. Gerhard Kittel, *Theological Dictionary of the New Testament,* 1:361 (section 3).

2. Ibid., p. 362.

3. A.T. Robertson, *Word Pictures in the New Testament,* 6:39.

4. F. de Sassure, "Course in General Linguistics" (translated from French) 1959, p. 69.

5. Ibid., p. 71.

6. Ludwig Wittgenstein, *Philosophical Investigations,* 3rd Ed., 1968, Part 1, p. 79.

7. Kittel, 4:282.

8. Ibid., pp. 113-5b.

Chapter Five

1. *Encylopaedia Britannica,* 15:919.